Compact Guide: Vietnam is the ideal quick-reference guide to the Land of the Ascending Dragon. It tells you all you need to know about the country's attractions, from the streets and markets of Hanoi to the beaches of the Central Coast, from the glorious monuments of Hue to the wonders of Halong Bay, and from the bustle of Saigon to the delta of the Mekong.

This is one of 120 Compact Guides, which combine the interests and enthusiasms of two of the world's best known information providers: Insight Guides, whose titles have set the standard for visual travel guides since 1970, and Discovery Channel, the world's premier source of nonfiction television programming.

Star Attractions

An instant reference to some of Vietnam's top attractions to help you set your priorities.

Hanoi p20

Water Puppet Theatre p24

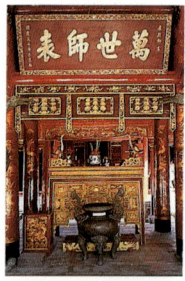
Temple of Literature p27

Halong Bay p36

Train to Lao Cai p38

Hue p41

Thien Mu Pagoda p45

Hoi An p51

Cham Towers p56

Cao Dai p67

Mekong River p69

Vietnam

Contents

Introduction

Vietnam – Land of the Ascending Dragon **5**
Historical Highlights **16**

Places

Route 1: Around Hanoi **20**
  Excursions from Hanoi **31**
Route 2: Haiphong and Halong Bay **35**
Route 3: Sapa and Dien Bien Phu **38**
Route 4: Hue and Environs **41**
Route 5: Hue to Da Nang and Hoi An **49**
Route 6: Champa and Central Coast **54**
Route 7: Dalat **58**
Route 8: Ho Chi Minh City (Saigon) **60**
  Excursions from Ho Chi Minh City **66**
Route 9: The Mekong Delta **69**

Culture

Vietnamese Temple Architecture **73**
Music and Theatre **74**
Festivals **75**

Leisure

Food and Drink **77**
Nightlife **81**
Shopping **82**
Active Holidays **83**

Practical Information

Getting There **85**
Getting Around **86**
Facts for the Visitor **88**
Accommodation **92**

Index **96**

Vietnam – Land of the Ascending Dragon

Opposite: ride on a dragon

For over two thousand years Vietnam's development as a nation has been marked by one immovable and unalterable factor – the proximity of China. The Middle Kingdom looms large in the history of Dai Viet. The relationship between the Vietnamese and the Chinese is in many ways a family affair, with all the closeness of shared values and bitterness of close rivalries. No country in Southeast Asia is culturally closer to China than Vietnam, and no other country in the region has spent so long fending off Chinese domination, often at a terrible cost in lives, economic development and political compromise.

Perhaps because of the long years of rivalry, Vietnam has developed a powerful sense of national identity, placing the Viets somewhere between China and the remainder of Southeast Asia – possessors of a unique cultural heritage which is both strongly Sinicised, yet also distinctively Southeast Asian. Thus most Vietnamese consider themselves Buddhists, but are followers of the Mahayana doctrine as taught in China rather than the Theravada school of nearby Thailand, Laos, Cambodia and Burma. Traditional Vietnamese values respect and closely adhere to the teachings of Confucius, whilst many Viets also revere the Way of Taoism. Yet they also believe in locality spirits and practise a distinctly Southeast Asian form of spirit worship. As long ago as the Tang Dynasty (6th to 9th centuries AD) Vietnamese fighters, engaged in yet another bout of struggle with the Chinese, sang a martial song which emphasised this separate identity in the clearest of terms:

> *Fight to keep our hair long,*
> *Fight to keep our teeth black,*
> *Fight so that the heroic southern country*
> *can never be defeated.*

Nowadays the Vietnamese may have trimmed their hair and turned to toothpaste instead of betel nut, but they remain as firmly devoted as ever to the concept of national independence and a distinct Viet cultural identity. At different times this has been both their country's weakness, and its strength. Long centuries of fighting the Chinese were followed, in the 19th and 20th centuries, by the experience – in close succession – of French colonialism, Japanese occupation and American intervention. Surely, by the time the communists finally attained victory in 1975, foreigners of all kinds must have seemed aggressive and untrustworthy to the victors!

Yet Vietnam could not stand alone. Within a few short months of achieving its decisive victory, Hanoi was once

Water traffic

Shrine at the Perfume Pagoda near Hanoi

Tools of the trade at Dien Bien Phu

again threatened by a dogmatic and expansionist Khmer Rouge regime in 'Democratic Kampuchea', backed by the old enemy, China, to the north. The apparent solution, an alliance with the Soviet Union and its allies, proved hardly more appealing. The Soviets behaved not unlike 'poor Americans', having far smaller purse-strings than the US, but making similar demands for naval facilities at Cam Ranh Bay and special status elsewhere in Vietnam. To make matters worse, all too often they behaved in a condescending or boorish manner. A journalist's account from the 1980s – burly Russians bargaining earnestly with a despairing Vietnamese shopkeeper as they try to exchange a piece of antique blue and white porcelain for bundles of Soviet calendars – sums up much of what was wrong with the relationship.

Today, most Vietnamese are anxious to put the years of war and privation behind them. Looking westwards to their Thai near neighbours, they see the manifold benefits that international tourism can bring, but they are also darkly aware of the problems. The Vietnamese authorities very much want to attract the hard currency associated with tourism, but worry about the 'negative impact' such visitors can bring. On the surface, the problems associated with tourism and a more open society are broadly represented as those of loose morals, drugs, anti-social behaviour and Aids, but truth to tell the aparatchiks who control the party machine are more concerned with the threat of open debate, a free press and genuine opposition.

Aids warning

Still, in the 10 years since Vietnam first began to open up to the outside world, great changes have indeed been made. Standards of accommodation have improved, thousands of new restaurants have opened, communications have improved and almost the whole country is now accessible. Still more importantly, as the regime has relaxed so have the Vietnamese people. Once characterised by a certain shyness or lack of security which sometimes manifested itself in a cool or reserved manner, the Vietnamese people are now increasingly open, friendly and eager to meet with foreign travellers. In truth they are eager to teach and eager to learn – so a visit to Vietnam at the start of the 21st century can indeed be a rewarding and remarkable experience.

Position and size

Slightly larger than Norway, Vietnam stretches over 1,600km (1000 miles) from north to south and from as little as 50km (32 miles) from east to west. The Socialist Republic of Vietnam, as it is officially known, covers an area of 329,566 sq km (127,245 sq miles). Vietnam's northernmost point lies just below the Tropic of Cancer, and its

southern extreme just above latitude 8°N. It shares land borders with China to the north and Laos and Cambodia to the west. In addition, Vietnam has a 3,450-km (2,150-mile) coastline on the South China Sea in the east. The capital, Hanoi, is located in the heart of the Red River Valley, in the north of the country, and the traditional heartland of the Viet people. The largest city, Saigon – since 1975 called Ho Chi Minh City – dominates the broad Mekong Delta in the south of the country, which forms the nation's rice bowl.

Incense spirals in Saigon

Crossing the Red River

Climate

Vietnam's location in the Southeast Asian monsoon zone, between the Tropic of Cancer and the Equator, gives rise to a complex and humid climate that varies from region to region. The average temperature of 22°C (72°F) varies slightly from one season to another.

Northern Vietnam's climate is influenced by the winds of Central Asia, which give rise to a climate similar to that of southern China. From November to April, the northern part of the country experiences a relatively cold and humid winter. Temperatures often fall as low as freezing point in the mountains lying north and west of Hanoi. Summer, between May and October, sees higher temperatures, heavy rain and sometimes typhoons. Both the north and centre experience their hottest months during June, July and August.

Southern Vietnam's climate is characterised by relatively constant temperatures, a rainy season between May and October, a relatively dry season from November to February, and a hot season between February and April, when temperatures may reach 35°C (95°F). The rains, brought by the Southwest Monsoon, are usually heavy. During this period, humidity rises to between 80 and 100 percent and conditions can be sticky and uncomfortable.

Home in the rain

Giao sisters near Sapa

Ethnic headgear

Cham sculpture at My Son

Population and religion

About 90 percent of the population are ethnic Viets, also known as Kinh. It is likely that they are descended from a number of diverse ethnic groups. Foremost amongst these were the Hung, also known as Lac, who practised intensive wet rice cultivation in the fertile Red River Delta. Over the centuries the Viets developed a southwards territorial imperative, pushed by their expanding numbers and channelled south by the all-but-impenetrable walls of the Annamite Cordillera. This move to the south added a Malayo-Polynesian element both to Viet ethnicity and to the Vietnamese language.

Vietnam's 1 million Chinese constitute the most important minority group. Only a few thousand have retained Chinese nationality, while the rest, known as Hoa, have adopted Vietnamese nationality. Their largest concentration is in the south, especially at Cholon and in the Mekong Delta. As elsewhere in Southeast Asia, they excel at business and are predominantly urban.

Ethnic Khmer, who live mainly in the Mekong Delta, number around 500,000; they are ethnically identical to the Khmers of Cambodia (by whom they are called *khmer krom*, or 'Lower Khmer').

The Cham inhabit the Phan Rang and Phan Thiet regions, as well as the Mekong Delta. Once masters of the central coast, they are now reduced to as few as 120,000 people. The coastal Cham are predominantly Hindu, whilst those of the Mekong Delta are Muslim.

Ethnic minorities living in the mountainous regions in central and southern Vietnam form another important group. Called Montagnards by the French, these tribes include Muong, Ra De, Jarai, Banhar and Sedang living in the Central Highlands. Totalling around 700,000 people, they have long resisted Viet influence and have only recently begun to integrate a little more into national life.

The highlands of northwestern Vietnam are home to many ethnic minorities. These include the Tay, who number just over a million and are found in the provinces of Cao Bang, Lang Son, Bac Thai, Quang Ninh, Ha Giang, and Tuyen Quang. Their villages are located in irrigated valleys where they build traditional stilt houses. They cultivate wet paddy rice, soya beans, cinnamon, tea, tobacco, cotton, indigo and a variety of fruits. Other important upland minorities of northwestern Vietnam include the Tai, close relations to the various Tai-speaking groups of Laos, Thailand and China's Yunnan Province, as well as the Hmong and the Nung.

Tea harvest

Most Vietnamese would describe themselves as Buddhists, but theirs is a very different Buddhism to that practised elsewhere in mainland Southeast Asia. Buddhism came to Vietnam from the north, by way of China, as did the other major belief systems of the Vietnamese, Confucianism and Taoism. The resultant mix, combined with an indigenous tradition of spirit worship, makes Vietnamese spiritual values both complex and unique.

Buddhism

Most ethnic Viets are Mahayana Buddhists, following the 'Greater Vehicle' interpretation of Buddhism, which places emphasis on attaining perfect wisdom and, ultimately, becoming a *bodhissatva* – that is, one who has achieved enlightenment but eschews nirvana, preferring instead to remain behind and help others follow the Noble Eightfold Path. In the south, and especially in the Mekong Delta, the ethnic Khmer are also Buddhists, but follow the older Theravada form of Buddhism which places emphasis on becoming an *arhat*, or saint, attaining enlightenment and achieving extinction. In practice, both Viet and Khmer Buddhists strive to do good in this life in the hope of being reborn into a better position.

Starting young

Confucianism

The teachings of Confucius – Khong Tu in Vietnamese – also derive from China, where the great philosopher K'ung Fu-tzu (551–478BC) taught a system of morals and ethical principles which guided Chinese (and subsequently Vietnamese) society for more than two millennia, and which still today underlie many values in both countries. Essentially, Confucianism emphasises filial piety, correct behaviour and loyal service in a society where the ruler maintains power by example rather than through force.

Taoism

The principles of Taoism, once again, are derived from China, where the philosopher Lao Tzu taught his doctrine

Christ statue above Vung Tau

Followers of Cao Dai

Cham Muslims

of *dao* – literally 'The Way' – in the 6th century BC. Taoism emphasises the duality of the universe based on a tension of opposing but complimentary forces, Yin and Yang, the female and male principles. The essence of Taoism is to preserve this natural balance through complex rituals and practices such as feng shui or geomancy.

Christianity

Chiefly through the efforts of Jesuit missionaries and the country's long association with France, Vietnam has an estimated 8 million Christians – after the Philippines, the largest number in Southeast Asia – most of whom live in the south. Of these around 95 percent are Catholics, the remainder being more recent converts to Protestantism, often minority peoples living in the Central Highlands.

Cao Dai and Hoa Hao

Vietnam has two indigenous religious sects, both of which were established in the 20th century, and both of which are based firmly in the south of the country. Cao Dai is the larger, with an estimated 2 million followers. With its Holy See at Tay Ninh to the northwest of Ho Chi Minh City, Cao Dai is an interesting and eclectic amalgam of Confucianism, Taoism, Buddhism and Catholicism. The second sect, called Hoa Hao or 'Peace and Happiness', is centred on Chau Doc in the Mekong Delta. Its followers practise an ascetic and austere form of Buddhism.

Hinduism and Islam

Hinduism was once a major religion in the region that constitutes modern Vietnam, but with the extinction of the Kingdom of Champa, it went into near terminal decline. Indeed, even whilst Champa survived it was already threatened by Buddhism and by Islam, both of which made serious inroads amongst the Chams. Today, followers of Hinduism are limited to a few urban South Asians and perhaps 60,000 Chams in and around Nha Trang and Phan Thiet. There are rather more Muslims, perhaps 80,000 Chams, living mainly in the Mekong Delta, as well as small communities of Chulia or Tamil-speaking Muslims in Hanoi and Ho Chi Minh City.

Language

The Vietnamese language is a fusion of Mon-Khmer, Tai and Chinese elements. Linguists consider that the original base was Mon-Khmer, a non-tonal language family from which modern Cambodian is derived, and from which Vietnamese acquired a significant proportion of its base vocabulary. To this over the centuries was added tonality and grammatical structure adapted from the neighbouring Tai-speaking peoples, and finally an extensive

Signs of the times

vocabulary, especially in the realms of philosophy, literature and political administration, from Chinese. Vietnamese is not an easy language for the foreign visitor to acquire; it requires long and intensive study to learn properly. It's easy enough to acquire some basic vocabulary, however – particularly useful are food and travel terminology – and, as always, this is greatly appreciated by the locals. The good news is that French is quite widely spoken in urban areas by older people, whilst English is burgeoning – young people everywhere are only too pleased to get in some practice. On a slightly more esoteric note, Chinese – both Mandarin and Guangdong – is making something of a comeback after years of repression, whilst Russian is fast disappearing.

Written Vietnamese
Chinese influence during the first centuries of Vietnam's history led to the extensive use of characters known as *chu nho,* thought to have replaced an ancient written script of Indic origin, a derivative of which is used today by the ethnic Muong minority. Even after independence in the 10th century, all manuscripts and government documents were written in *chu nho.* In time scholars realised the necessity and advantages of developing a separate written Vietnamese language. Several tentative attempts were made to modify Chinese characters, but it was not until the 13th century that the esteemed poet Nguyen Thuyen managed to evolve a distinct though complex script called *chu nom.* Although standardised for popular literature, *chu nom* never received official recognition, and most Vietnamese scholars continued to use Chinese characters. A sea change came in the mid-17th century when Alexandre de Rhodes, a French Jesuit missionary, developed a Romanised script known as *quoc ngu*. Initially, use of this system was confined to the Catholic church and – after

Browsing for books

Chinese characters

about 1860 – the colonial administration. The study of *quoc ngu* became compulsory in secondary schools in 1906, and two years later, the royal court in Hue ordered a new curriculum, written entirely in *quoc ngu*. It became the national written language in 1919.

Politics and administration

In July 1976, following the victory of the communist North in the Second Indochina War, Vietnam was officially reunified. A radical programme of socialist construction was put forward, calling for the rapid socialisation of the defeated South, with the forced collectivisation of agriculture, small industry and commerce. This soon led to economic disaster, prompting waves of refugees – the tragic 'boat people' – to flee the country. On the international front, in early 1977 Vietnam found itself in conflict with Pol Pot's Cambodia and on a collision course with its old enemy, China. As a consequence, in 1978 Vietnam signed a security pact with COMECON and the former Soviet Union. Once again, Vietnam was entangled in great power rivalries and the politics of the Cold War.

The invasion of Cambodia in December 1978 and the subsequent Chinese invasion in early 1979 augured a new cycle of struggle, which – combined with disastrous socialist economic policies at home – spelled gradual financial collapse for the struggling Vietnamese state. Vietnam was isolated internationally, tied into a failing Soviet power bloc, and engaged in fighting a protracted war against the elusive Cambodian resistance.

At the Sixth Party Congress in 1986, following the Soviet example of *glasnost* and *perestroika,* the party finally decided to launch the country on an ambitious programme of social and economic reform called *doi moi*. Collectivisation of land was rolled back, and a new emphasis was placed on the individual peasant. As a consequence, agricultural production increased, and rice harvests in particular burgeoned. Political controls remained tight, however, and little reign was given to individual rights of expression.

Between 1989 and 1991 the Vietnamese leadership was deeply shaken first by the events in Beijing's Tiananmen Square, then – to the very roots of their ideology – by the collapse of the Soviet Union and the dismantling of communism in Eastern Europe. Political solidarity aside, they had lost in one fell swoop all their major financial and economic backers. The country was technically bankrupt, mired in Cambodia, and increasingly sidelined internationally. Something had to be done.

Hanoi responded by negotiating a withdrawal from Cambodia with the United Nations, and cautiously opening the doors to foreign investment. Western nations –

Out in force at the Tet Festival

Past heroes remembered

notably France and the European Union – were keen to test the waters, but not until early 1994 did the United States lift its punitive embargo and permit economic and cultural exchanges with Vietnam. Meanwhile, Vietnam's new face had struck a responsive cord with its Southeast Asian neighbours. As a result, after short but intensive negotiations, Vietnam became a full member of ASEAN in 1995.

Today the Communist Party's aim is to retain its firm grip on power as the country develops economically. The leaders are aging, yet there are no clear indications as to who is to replace them. Within the Party there are divisions of opinion, with some wishing to continue the liberalisation of the economy and opening the door to foreigners, whilst others pin their hopes on slowing down reform, fearing the party is losing control.

Visitor to Hue

For most of the 1990s the leadership had little to fear in the way of opposition. The economy was developing erratically but steadily, sometimes at rates of as much as 8 percent a year. Standards of living were low, but were clearly improving. Rice exports were on the increase, the country was at peace, and there seemed to be light at the end of the tunnel.

The Asian economic crisis of 1997 changed all that. Suddenly Southeast Asia's booming economies were in regression, with regional currencies falling in value and export figures in negative growth. Talk of Vietnam becoming Asia's next 'tiger economy' now seems premature, to say the least. But what of the future? Vietnam is a fertile land blessed with great natural resources as well as a shrewd, hard-working and ambitious population. Shielded by the remnants of its faltering command economy, the country seems so far to have weathered the Asian economic downfall comparatively well. If the path to political reform remains unobstructed and the economics of the free market are fully espoused, Vietnam seems bound to prosper. After all the years of suffering and sacrifice, it certainly deserves to do so.

Economy

The Vietnamese economy suffers, and for some years is likely to continue to suffer, from the long years of war, sterile socialist command economics, and suspicion of capitalism both domestic and foreign. Following the *doi moi* economic liberalisation of the early 1990s, great things were expected but, by and large, have only partly materialised. Vietnam's gross domestic product surged in the early 1990s, but then fell back, weakened both by the sclerosis of party control and by widespread graft and corruption in both administration and the workplace. The problem was compounded by the Asian economic collapse of 1997, with Vietnam seriously affected by the falling

Tending the crop

New hope

Rush hour in Hanoi

Woman at work

currencies and declining exports across the region. Economic disparity between town and countryside is high and growing fast, and disillusion with party interference in the supposedly free market economy is widespread.

The streets of the capital, Hanoi, and especially the largest city, Ho Chi Minh City, still bustle with enthusiasm and business energy. The abandonment of socialist economics and its gradual replacement by limited market-oriented capitalism has been welcomed by the populace. People everywhere are angling to make money, and the streets are filled with small-scale private enterprises selling cheap consumer goods. Yet the country is still poor. About 40 percent of the population are undernourished. Unemployment is on the rise. Whilst almost everyone has some kind of job, an increasing number of people are underemployed. Nearly every household in the cities has a TV set, but fewer than 10 percent do in the countryside. Motorcycles are the vehicle of choice in urban areas, but are rare in the countryside where most people work. The state sector has been trimming jobs and eliminating whole sectors, driving up unemployment. The over-large and antiquated military is being down-sized, whilst the population is young and growing. Pressure on the labour market is huge and continuing to grow.

Workers are comparatively well-educated and learn quickly, but they are not yet highly skilled, requiring foreign firms to invest in training. The government remains cautious and conservative, apparently unwilling to allow the free market full reign. Privatisation remains a dirty word, and although foreign investment has seen some limited success, the state sector seems reluctant to relinquish its stranglehold on key sectors of the economy. Corruption remains rampant, salaries are low, and the old men in power remain deeply suspicious of foreign intentions.

Nature and environment

Vietnam is regarded as one of Asia's most biologically diverse countries, an evolutionary hotspot. The Vu Quang wildlife reserve has even been described as 'the Galápagos of Southeast Asia', with various previously unknown flora and fauna still being discovered. Habitats range from the mountainous Central Highlands to the long, extended coastline, and from the flat, marshy Mekong Delta to the cool, high mountains of the country's northwest. The wild fauna includes 275 species of mammal, 180 reptiles, 80 amphibious species, 773 bird species, hundreds of fish and thousands of invertebrate species. Plant life is even more varied, with around 7,000 plant species. Over 2,000 of these are used for food, medicine, animal fodder and timber.

Unfortunately the all too common problems of deforestation and burgeoning population have placed enormous pressure on the country's natural resources, an environment already severely crippled by 30 years of war. During the Second Indochina War, over 72 million litres of herbicides were dropped over much of southern Vietnam. Over 2 million hectares of forest and farmland were lost to defoliation and bombing.

In 1943 more than 40 percent of the land was covered with forest, but by 1995 that figure was just 19 percent. Recently, however, it has risen to 28 percent as a result of the government's banning of unprocessed timber products and an active reforestation programme.

Wildlife

Over the past decade, scientists have discovered three new large mammals in Vietnam's remote forests. This is an astonishing statistic when one considers that fewer than 10 new large mammals have been discovered in the 20th century anywhere in the world. The most recent discovery, the Truong Son muntjac, follows the saola or Vu Quang ox found in 1992 and the giant muntjac in 1994.

Other large mammals found in Vietnam include the tiger, leopard, banteng, kouprey, Asian elephant and gaur. All these animals are regarded as endangered. Endemic Vietnamese species include the Tonkin snub-nosed monkey, Edward's pheasant and Vo Quy's pheasant.

The government has set up various national parks as well as marine conservation sites. They include the Bach Ma National Park in the Central Highlands, and Cat Tien National Park in southern Vietnam. Bach Ma's inhabitants include the elusive clouded leopard and the endemic and very rare Annamensis Hill Partridge. Cat Tien is one of only two places in the world where Javan rhinos are known to exist. Hon Mun Marine Park in Nha Trang is now one of Vietnam's foremost snorkelling and scuba diving sites.

Deforestation is still a problem

Mountain flora

Dien Bien Phu

Historical Highlights

Legendary period King De Minh, descendant of a divine Chinese ruler, marries an immortal mountain fairy. Their offspring, Kinh Duong, in turn marries the daughter of the Dragon Lord of the Sea. Their son, Lac Long Quan or 'Dragon Lord of Lac', is regarded as the first Vietnamese king. To maintain peace with the Chinese, Lac Long Quan marries Au Co, a Chinese immortal, who bears him 100 sons: the eldest succeeds him as the first king of the Hung (Hong Bang) Dynasty. The 18 kings of the Hung Dynasty each ruled for 150 years. During this time the southwards territorial imperative of both the Han Chinese and the Vietnamese was established.

258BC Thuc Pan, ruler of Au Viet, overthrows the 18th Hung king and establishes a new Vietnamese state called Au Lac, with its capital at Co Loa near present-day Hanoi.

207BC Trieu Da, a renegade Chinese general, conquers Au Lac and rules over Nam Viet, a state based on southern China and northern Vietnam.

111BC Chinese dominion over Vietnam is confirmed when the heirs of Trieu Da submit to the Han emperor Wu-Ti, establishing Chinese rule as far south as the Hai Van Pass. Nam Viet becomes the Chinese province of Giao Chau.

1st century AD Attempts made to Sinicise the inhabitants of Giao Chau provoke widespread popular hostility amongst the Vietnamese.

40AD The Trung Sisters lead a rebellion against the Chinese, proclaiming themselves queens of an independent Vietnam. Three years later a powerful Han army under General Ma Vien reestablishes Chinese control: the Trung sisters are martyred and Sinicisation is resumed.

43–938 Period of Chinese occupation, despite several attempts to reestablish independence.

544 Revolt led by Viet scholar Ly Bon results in setting up of Early Ly Dynasty (544–602).

603 Chinese reestablish control over Vietnam which they rename An Nam or 'Pacified South'. Chinese rule remains secure under the powerful Tang Dynasty (618–907).

938 General Ngo Quyen defeats the Chinese at the Bach Dang River and reasserts Vietnamese independence after a thousand years of Chinese domination. Ngo Quyen renames the country Dai Viet and establishes his capital at Co Loa, reaffirming spiritual continuity with ancient Au Lac.

939–65 Ngo Quyen dies in 945; Ngo Dynasty rapidly declines as power is divided between 12 competing principalities.

968 The most powerful of the 12 feudal lords, Dinh Bo Linh, reunifies the country and establishes the Dinh Dynasty (968–80). As Emperor Dinh Tien Hoang De, he maintains Vietnamese independence but agrees to pay tribute to China.

979 Dinh Tieng Hoang De assassinated; throne usurped by Le Dai Hanh, founder of the Early Le Dynasty (980–1009). Viet forces begin attacks on the Indianised state of Champa to the south.

1005 Buddhism spreads as major religion of Vietnam under the aegis of monk Khuong Viet.

1009–1225 Later Ly Dynasty consolidates the Vietnamese nation with their capital at Thang Long or 'Ascending Dragon' – later Hanoi. Buddhism established as state religion, Confucianism as basis for state administration. Van Mieu (Temple of Literature) founded at Hanoi in 1070.

1225–1400 Tran Dynasty. Buddhism increasingly mixed with Confucian and Taoist doctrines. In 1279 General Tran Hung Dao defeats Mongol invaders at the second Battle of the Bach Dang River. Viet expansion in the south continues. Hue region of central Annam absorbed.

1400–07 Ambitious minister Ho Qui Ly manoeuvres himself to power and founds short-lived Ho Dynasty. In 1407 Ming Chinese occupy country and attempt forced Sinicisation of the Viets.

1428–1788 Later Le Dynasty. National hero Le Loi drives out the Chinese and becomes King Le Thai To. Consolidation of Dai Viet.

1471 Champa suffers crushing military defeat at the hands of King Le Thanh Ton; Vietnam's southern frontier pushed beyond Qui Nhon.

1516 Portuguese seafarers arrive in Vietnam.

1527 Mac Dang Dung seizes power in Hanoi. Rival Trinh and Nguyen Lords establish themselves further south. Le Dynasty retains nominal power until 1788.

1539–1787 Trinh Lords dominate the north, taking Hanoi from Macs in 1592. For most of the same period (1558–1778) Nguyen Lords dominate the south from their capital at Hue.

1627 Missionary Alexandre de Rhodes develops Romanised script for Vietnamese language.

1680–1757 Vietnamese southern expansion continues. Mekong Delta (including Prey Nokor, later Saigon) taken from Cambodia.

1776–92 Tay Son Rising: Nguyen Lords overthrown in 1777, Nguyen Anh escapes and seeks French assistance. Trinh Lords overthrown in 1787. Le Chieu Tong escapes and seeks Chinese assistance. Tay Sons defeat the Chinese and briefly unite the country. In 1788 Nguyen Anh gains control of Saigon; civil war with Tay Sons.

1802 Victorious Nguyen Anh founds Nguyen Dynasty (1802–1945) and proclaims himself Emperor Gia Long from capital at Hue.

1832 Last vestiges of Champa kingdom extinguished by Minh Mang.

1820–41 Minh Mang hostile to Christianity and growing French influence.

1858–9 France seizes Da Nang and Saigon.

1865 Cochinchina declared a French colony.

1883 France establishes protectorate over Annam and Tonkin. Nguyen emperors powerless.

1887 France creates Indochinese Union of Vietnam, Laos and Cambodia.

1890 Birth of Ho Chi Minh near Vinh.

1918 Ho Chi Minh travels to Paris, joins French Communist Party in 1920.

1930 Ho Chi Minh forms Indochinese Communist Party in Hong Kong.

1940 In September Japan occupies Indochina but leaves French colonial administration intact.

1941 Ho Chi Minh returns secretly to Vietnam and forms the Vietminh to fight for independence.

1945 March 9, Japan takes over French administration; March 11, Emperor Bao Dai proclaims independence under Japanese auspices; August 15, Japan capitulates; August 23, Bao Dai abdicates; September 2, Ho Chi Minh declares Vietnamese independence in Hanoi.

1946 First Indochina War begins as French seek to reimpose their rule.

1954 France suffers crushing defeat at Dien Bien Phu. Vietnam divided at 17th Parallel pending elections. North, the Democratic Republic of Vietnam, led by Ho Chi Minh. South, the Republic of Vietnam, under Ngo Dinh Diem.

1955 Diem refuses to hold elections. Viet Minh launch Second Indochina War in South.

1960 North Vietnam introduces conscription. First US advisers arrive in South.

1965 President Johnson starts to bomb North; first US combat troops land at Da Nang in South.

1968 US troop strength rises to 540,000, but Tet Offensive saps morale.

1969 Ho Chi Minh dies; US begins phased withdrawal of troops.

1973 Washington and Hanoi sign ceasefire.

1975 NVA capture Saigon. Vietnam reunified. US imposes trade embargo.

1976 Socialist Republic of Vietnam is declared. Communist regime in Cambodia begins territorial aggression.

1978 Vietnam invades Cambodia. The following year China retaliates by invading Vietnam.

1986 Start of *doi moi* socio-economic reforms.

1994 US trade embargo lifted. A year later, Vietnam joins ASEAN (Association of Southeast Asian Nations).

Daily routine in the Old Quarter

Preceding pages: landscape around Sa Pa

Part of the colonial legacy

Route 1

Hanoi *See map on page 22*

Hanoi is one of the best-kept secrets in Southeast Asia. Years of war and political isolation have combined to keep the Vietnamese capital off the tourist map – at least until fairly recently. Visitors will be surprised and delighted to find that Hanoi is probably the most beautiful capital city in Southeast Asia, combining indigenous architectural treasures with fine examples of French colonial architecture. The people are friendly, the food is excellent.

The area around Hanoi – the name means 'within the waters', a reference to the city's close relationship with the Song Hong, or 'Red River' and numerous surrounding lakes – has been the site of Vietnam's capital, on and off, for more than two millennia. In the 3rd century BC King Thuc Pan established the earliest Vietnamese capital at the citadel of Co Loa just north of the present-day city. Over a thousand years later, when the Chinese were driven out and independence restored, General Ngo Quyen symbolically chose Hanoi as the site of the reborn Vietnamese nation. Subsequently, in 1802, the first Nguyen Emperor, Gia Long, transferred the capital to Hue – but this proved to be a short-lived move. In 1902 France established Hanoi as the capital not just of Vietnam, but of all French Indochina. In 1954 the city became the capital of the communist north, and in 1976, following the defeat of the non-communist south, it was proclaimed capital of the reunited Socialist Republic of Vietnam. In many ways Hanoi remains the heart of the Vietnamese nation.

At the end of the 19th century, Hanoi was still a relatively small town, centred on the Old Quarter and the administrative area within the Citadel. While still not a

Southeast Asian megalopolis like Bangkok or Jakarta, over the intervening hundred years the Vietnamese capital has grown into a city of three million people, expanding southwards and westwards away from the Red River to encompass a broad region of lakeland. Here the French colonial rulers established their administrative and commercial quarters, and subsequently a free Vietnam built monuments to the struggle for independence and to the father of that independence, Ho Chi Minh.

City Tour 1 – Hanoi Old Quarter

There's no better place to start your acquaintance with Hanoi than the city's bustling Old Quarter. ★ **Ho Hoan Kiem** ❶ – 'the lake of the restored sword' – lies right in the centre of old Hanoi and holds a special place in the hearts of the Vietnamese. According to legend, the Viet hero Le Loi was given a magic sword with which to fight the Chinese by the Divine Turtle, which lives in Ho Hoan Kiem. After a 10-year struggle (1418–28), Le Loi drove out the Chinese invaders and, as Emperor Le Thai Tho (1428–33), restored the sword to its rightful owner beneath the tranquil waters of Hoan Kiem. Today the lake makes a delightful retreat from the bustle of central Hanoi. To the east of the lake, a path winds beneath shady trees, whilst to the west, groups of wispy-bearded old men spend their retirement playing chess. In the middle of the lake a small pagoda, **Thap Rua** or 'Tortoise Tower', stands on an islet. This Vietnamese folly – erected as recently as 1886 – looks best by night, illuminated by fairy lights.

The visitor should proceed north along Le Thai Tho by the western edge of the lake. A slight diversion west along Hang Trong leads to **St Joseph's Cathedral** ❷ (consecrated in 1886), a neo-Gothic building of no outstanding architectural merit, but an interesting souvenir of the French colonial period. By returning to the lake's shore and continuing north along Le Thai Tho, the visitor will enter Hanoi's fascinating ★ **Old Quarter**, also known as 36 *Pho Puong*, or the '36 Streets'. This area, which is almost entirely devoted to commerce, dates back to the 13th century when a group of 36 guilds established themselves here, each centred on a particular street. Today many of the street names still survive, although only a few are still readily identifiable by trade. In Vietnamese *hang* means 'merchandise', thus *Hang Bac* has come to mean 'Silver Street', which even today specialises in selling jewellery.

Other examples include *Hang Chieu* or 'Mat Street', *Hang Ma* or 'Paper Street', and *Hang Thiec* or 'Tin Street', all of which still market the speciality their name implies. By contrast *Hang Quat*, which used to sell fans, now offers bright red flags, lacquerware and candlesticks,

The turtle and the sword

Thap Rua

Hang Quat Street

whilst *Hang Buom* or 'Sail Street' – an area long associated with Hanoi's Hoa, or Overseas Chinese community – now specialises in imported foods and confectionery, with nary a sail in sight.

The Old Quarter is also remarkable for its traditional 'tube houses' – long, narrow commercial buildings designed to combine shop front, storage space and living quarters – which may be as narrow as 2m (6ft) across, but as much as 50m (162ft) deep. Designed in this fashion in the 15th century to minimise taxation on shop frontage, they have survived only in Hanoi's merchant quarter and in the ancient town of Hoi An. The best way to see the Old Quarter is to ramble almost at random, seeking out the most lively or fascinating sights, yet moving in a generally northwards direction towards busy **Dong Xuan Market ❸**. The largest market in Hanoi, Dong

Dong Xuan Market

Xuan is named after an ancient hamlet long since absorbed within the city. Built in 1889 by the French administration to replace the older Cau Dung or 'Eastern Bridge' market, Dong Xuan was destroyed by fire in 1994, but has since been rebuilt and retains its original façade.

Leaving Dong Xuan to its bustling fruit and vegetable merchants, continue north until you reach the railway line, then turn east along Pho Gam Cau until you reach the great embankment which holds back the Red River in time of spate. The long railway bridge spanning the river at this point is the famous **Long Bien Bridge** ❹, completed in 1902 and originally named after the then colonial governor of Indochina, Paul Doumer. During the Second Indochina War this bridge was of great strategic significance, providing the only communications link across the Red River to China. Defended by anti-aircraft guns and SAM missiles, it was repeatedly bombed by the Americans and doggedly repaired by the Vietnamese – hence the strange irregularity in the framework of rusty metal pylons and struts that support its 1700m (5,500ft) span.

Long Bien Bridge

Turn south from the bridge along busy Tran Nhat Duat and proceed to Hang Chieu, the third turning on the right. This leads back into the Old Quarter by way of **Cua O Quan Chuong**, the 'Gate of the Commander of the Garrison', built in 1749 and now the last of Old Hanoi's fortified gateways. From here it's just a short walk to the revered **Den Bach Ma** ❺ or 'White Horse Temple'. Founded in the 9th century by King Ly Thai in honour of a white horse guardian spirit that appeared to protect the Old City fortifications, the temple in its present form dates largely from the 18th century and fairly gleams with red lacquer and gilt. Even a brief glance is enough to suggest strong Chinese influence, and in fact Bach Ma was once associated with the veneration by the local Hoa community of Ma Vien, the Chinese general who defeated the Trung Sisters and subjugated Vietnam in 43AD.

Den Bach Ma interior

The route continues south through the narrow streets of the shoe bazaar emerging at the northeast corner of Ho Hoan Kiem. On a small mound nearby stands a tall, tapering stone column in the shape of a brush pen. This **Writing Brush Pillar**, which proclaims in Chinese characters *ta thanh thien* or 'writing on a blue sky', was designed by the revered 19th-century scholar Nguyen Van Sieu. Close by, the graceful, red-lacquered curve of **The Huc**, or 'Sunrise Bridge', leads to a small island and to ★ **Den Ngoc Son** ❻, the 'Temple of the Jade Mound'. This elegant building was founded in the 14th century and was originally a Confucian temple. In the 16th–18th centuries it served as a pleasure pavilion for the Trinh Lords of northern Vietnam, while in the 19th century it was reconstituted

Den Ngoc Son

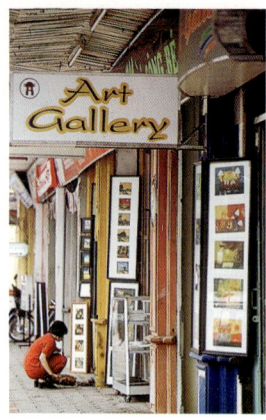

One of many art galleries

as a Buddhist temple. It is now primarily associated with the cult of deified warriors, most notably Tran Hung Dao, the general who defeated the Mongols at the Bach Dang River in 1279.

Cross back over the Huc Bridge and note the dilapidated concrete **Martyrs' Monument** erected to honour those who died fighting for the winning side in Vietnam's Indochina wars. Nearby, on the east of Pho Dinh Tien Hoang, is a fine old temple converted to serve as an art gallery, which certainly merits a visit. Indeed, the shop fronts along the northern and western sides of Hoa Hoan Kiem are dotted with **art galleries**. No other city in Southeast Asia has a better or more eclectic collection of galleries, offering everything from traditional Vietnamese art to European-style paintings – the influence, in particular, of Vietnam's French and Russian ties being readily apparent. This is a good area to stroll and shop in during the early evening, especially as there are numerous small restaurants and cafés where iced beer and excellent Vietnamese coffee are available. Young couples, too, favour this lakeside area for early evening trysts – generally executed with an elegant discretion.

24

Water Puppet performance

A puppeteer prepares

After taking some refreshment, be certain to round off the day by visiting the ★ **Water Puppet Theatre** ❼ at 57 Pho Dinh Tien Hoang, just opposite the eastern end of the Huc Bridge. Unlikely though it may sound, this is a truly remarkable art, being uniquely Vietnamese and genuinely impressive. Water puppetry – known in Vietnamese as *roi nuoc* – originated in the Red River Delta of northern Vietnam more than a thousand years ago and, as an art form, still remains unknown virtually everywhere else. The puppets are carved from the hard, water-resistant wood of the fig tree to represent both traditional rural lifestyles (farmers, buffaloes, ducks, officials) and mythical creatures (dragons, phoenixes, unicorns). Standing concealed behind the watery stage, themselves waist-deep in water, the puppeteers use a complicated but invisible system of pulleys and poles to manoeuvre their wooden charges. The special effects are very clever indeed; rice sprouts from the water at an accelerated pace and smoke and fire issues from the dragons' mouths. Meanwhile, puppet people and puppet farm animals appear to walk on water as they live out their everyday lives farming, hunting, fishing and flirting whilst attempting to avoid various kinds of misfortune. All the while a traditional orchestra playing flutes, drums, xylophones, gongs and stringed instruments provides appropriate accompanying music. Performances are held 8–9pm every day except Monday. Shows are popular, so it is wise to book in advance.

City Tour 2 – Downtown Hanoi

Tran Quoc Pagoda

A good place to start a tour of Downtown Hanoi's lakes, temples and pagodas is the **Tran Quoc Pagoda** ❽, picturesquely situated on an island to the west of the causeway which separates Truc Bach Lake from the much larger Ho Tay, or **West Lake**. From Tran Quoc it is easy to appreciate the key role which the shifting waters of the Red River have played in the shaping of the Vietnamese capital over the centuries. Tran Quoc – 'Defend the Nation' – Pagoda is one of Vietnam's oldest temples, possibly dating back to the 6th century Early Ly Dynasty. A stone stele of 1639 still preserved in the temple grounds records that it was relocated in the 15th century to protect it from the encroaching Red River. In its current elegant and rather restrained form it dates from 1842.

West Lake

From Tran Quoc walk or take a taxi south along Duong Thanh Nien causeway. To the east lie the still waters of Truc Bach or 'White Silk' Lake. During the 18th century the Trinh Lords built a summer palace here, which was later transformed into a place of detention for errant royal concubines, who were obliged to weave a particularly fine white silk – hence the name of the lake. Turn east on leaving the causeway and enter the quiet and shaded grounds of **Quan Thanh Temple** ❾, endowed by the founder of the Early Ly Dynasty, Ly Thai To, in the early 11th century. The temple – which has been rebuilt several times, most recently in 1893 – is dedicated to Tran Vo, Guardian of the North, who protects the city from malevolent influences. An image of this Taoist divinity, accompanied by his symbols of power, the turtle and the snake, cast in black bronze by Trum Trong in 1677, stands nearly 4m (13ft) high on the main altar. A statue of the celebrated master craftsman stands to one side.

On leaving this temple, continue south along Duong Hung Vuong Boulevard, passing, on the west side, Hanoi

Inside Ho Chi Minh's House

Ho Chi Minh Mausoleum

Botanical Gardens and the **Presidential Palace**, the latter a beautifully restored example of French colonial architecture originally constructed in 1906 as the Palace of the Governor General of Indochina. Although closed to the public – nowadays it is used to receive visiting heads of state – it is possible to walk through the palace grounds by a clearly indicated route to visit **Ho Chi Minh's House** ❿ (Tuesday to Sunday 8–11am and 1.30–4.30pm), an unassuming residence raised on stilts where Ho spent the last decade of his life. The house is airy, with a neat garden beside a small pond. On the first floor Ho's bedroom and study are preserved as he left them – clean, simple and somewhat spartan.

Immediately to the south lies the symbolic heart of the Socialist Republic of Vietnam, with the **Ho Chi Minh Mausoleum** (Tuesday to Thursday 8–11am; usually closed October to December) facing the National Assembly across Ba Dinh Square. It was in this square that Ho read the Vietnamese Declaration of Independence on 2 September 1945, and it is here that he was entombed several years after his death on 2 September 1969. The mausoleum, a monolithic grey structure built in the Stalinist style, was constructed in 1973–5, using marble, granite and rare woods brought from all over Vietnam. Visitors may enter and view Ho's embalmed body, but only briefly as military guards keep the line of visitors moving swiftly along. It is essential to dress correctly. Cameras and bags must be left at the reception hall.

One Pillar Pagoda

On leaving the mausoleum continue south for about 200m (650ft) before turning west along Chua Mot Cot, the road named for Hanoi's famous ★ **One Pillar Pagoda**. Chua Mot Cot, a small but elegant wooden pagoda built by King Ly Thai Tong (1028–54) of the Early Ly Dynasty. According to tradition, Quan The Am Bo Tat, better known as Kuan Yin, the Goddess of Mercy, appeared to the heirless king in a dream. Seated on a lotus throne, she handed him a baby boy. Soon after Ly Thai Tong married a young peasant girl who bore him a son and heir. To commemorate this event and give thanks to the Goddess, Ly Thai Tong ordered the construction of Chua Mot Kot, in the shape of a lotus flower, in 1049. The single column on which the pagoda rests in a tranquil lotus pond represents the 'stem' of the temple. The bo tree behind the temple was planted by President Nehru of India during a state visit in 1958 and is said to be an offshoot of the one under which the Buddha attained enlightenment. The attractive façade of the nearby **Dien Huu Pagoda** opens onto a quiet garden courtyard – a good place for a contemplative moment, though many Vietnamese visitors come for the acupuncture treatment with which the temple is associated.

Close by – indeed so close that it dominates both pagodas – is the **Ho Chi Minh Museum** ⓫ (daily 8–11am, 1.30–4.30pm), which opened on 19 May 1990, the centenary of Ho's birth. Exhibits concentrate on Ho's life, the development of the Vietnamese revolution, and displays of the great leader's personal effects.

After visiting the museum, head back east along Chua Mot Cot Road until you reach Dien Bien Phu, a long boulevard of shady trees and gingerbread colonial buildings, nearly all of which have been restored in recent years. After about half a kilometre, opposite the Lenin Monument, stands the **Army Museum** ⓬ (Tuesday to Sunday 8–11am, 1.30–4.30pm). This merits a visit, providing well-presented displays of Vietnamese military history, essentially during the struggle for independence and the subsequent war in the south. The museum courtyard – which is full of weaponry from the Indochinese Wars including a Russian MIG 21 fighter – marks the southwestern corner of the **Citadel**, formerly the centre of administration in pre-colonial times and today a restricted military area in the heart of Hanoi. Fortunately ★ **Cot Co Flag Tower** ⓭, which is perhaps the most interesting feature of the Citadel, is open to the public and well worth the climb for the views over the city to the Red River and the Long Bien Bridge.

Army Museum exhibits

From Cot Co head south past the Lenin Monument and the Chinese Embassy until you reach busy Nguyen Thai Hoc. Turn west and walk a short distance to the **National Fine Arts Museum** (Tuesday to Sunday 8am–noon, 1.30–4.30pm) which offers displays of art history from Dong Son, through the Kingdom of Champa and the pre-colonial Vietnamese dynasties, to more recent – but fast disappearing – Socialist Realism.

Just across Nguyen Thai Hoc, heading due south, is the smaller Van Mieu Road which leads to the ★★ **Temple of Literature** or **Van Mieu** ⓮, one of Vietnam's foremost cultural treasures. Founded in 1070 by King Ly Thanh Tong of the Early Ly Dynasty, the temple was originally dedicated both to Confucius and to Chu Cong, a member of the Chinese royal family credited with originating many of the teachings that Confucius developed 500 years later. The site was selected by Ly Dynasty geomancers to stand in harmony with the Taoist Bich Cau temple and the Buddhist One Pillar Pagoda, representing the three major fonts of Vietnamese tradition. Six years later, in 1076, the Quoc Tu Giam, or 'School for the Sons of the Nation', was established at the same location when King Ly Nhan Tong (1072–1127) founded Vietnam's first university. The tradition of Confucian education flourished at the Temple of Literature, with the custom of offering

Temple of Literature

Cot Co Flag Tower

Strolling in the Temple grounds

a cloak to successful candidates beginning in 1374, whilst in 1484 the first stele bearing the names of doctoral graduates was erected. After 1802, however, with the establishment of the Nguyen Dynasty and the removal of the capital to Hue, the Royal University was moved too. The Van Mieu continued to function, but the Quoc Tu Giam buildings were turned into a shrine to the parents of Confucius called Khai Thanh. The last regional examinations held at the Temple of Literature were conducted in 1915.

The French – who demolished numerous historical buildings in the region when building their new administrative quarter at the turn of the 19th century – appreciated the unique significance of the temple complex and made it a protected historical building in 1906. Nevertheless, in 1947, at the beginning of the First Indochina War, French shells demolished both Khai Thanh and the Houses of the Disciples in the Courtyard of the Sages. The Vietnamese clearly learned a lesson from this disaster, for during the Second Indochina War many precious objects at the Temple of Literature were put into storage, whilst the stelae were buried in sand and surrounded by a reinforced concrete wall as protection against stray American bombs. In 1988, as a consequence of liberalisation, the statues of Confucius and his disciples were restored to the temple and the complex opened to public viewing.

Entry to the complex is through **Van Mieu Gate**. The layout, modelled on that of the temple at Qufu in China's Shandong Province where Confucius was born, consists of a succession of five walled courtyards. The first two courtyards, joined by **Dai Trung Mon** or 'Great Middle Gate', are carefully maintained gardens of tranquillity in the heart of Downtown Hanoi where locals come to paint, read or converse quietly in the shade of the trees. The third

Waiting at the Van Mieu Gate

courtyard is reached via **Khue Van Cac** or 'Pavilion of the Constellation of Literature', a fine double-roofed gateway built in 1805. Here the visitor will find the '**Garden of Stelae**' – 82 stone memorials mounted on the backs of tortoises, each listing the names and brief biographical details of graduates of the Temple of Literature dating back to the 15th century – a total of 1,306 scholars. In the centre of the courtyard is a walled pond called **Thien Quang Tinh**, or 'The Well of Heavenly Clarity'.

Entry to the fourth courtyard, or Courtyard of the Sages, is via **Dai Thanh Mon**, or 'Gate of the Great Synthesis'. It was here, in the **Great House of Ceremonies**, that in times past the king would make offerings at the **Altar to Confucius** while new university graduates would kneel and prostrate themselves to pay respect. Behind the Great House of the Ceremonies is the **Sanctuary** with statues of Confucius and his leading disciples including Manh Tu or Mencius. Flanking the courtyard to east and west were once altars to the Houses of the Disciples of Confucius, but these were destroyed in the shelling of 1947 and have been replaced by a shop, a small museum and administrative offices. This courtyard is still used for chess games using people as live chess pieces, and for ceremonial dances, during the Tet festivities. It is also possible to listen to traditional Vietnamese music here. The fifth and final courtyard once housed the Royal University and, following the transfer of the capital to Hue in 1802, the **Khai Thanh** shrine to Confucius's parents. Again, and most unfortunately, these buildings were destroyed by shelling in 1947. At present the fifth courtyard contains the **Lieu Hanh Shrine**, dedicated to the goddess who is one of the 'Four Immortals' honoured by Vietnamese tradition.

About 250m southwest of Van Mieu on Bich Cau Street is ★ **Dao Quan Bich Cau**, or Bich Cau Taoist temple, the third temple in the symbolic geomantic triangle of the Ly Kings, together with Confucian Van Mieu and Buddhist Chua Mot Cot. One of the most attractive structures in Hanoi, Bich Cau was re-dedicated to the Immortal Ta Uyen who helped King Le Thanh Ton inflict a crushing military defeat on the Kingdom of Champa in 1471. Bich Cau consists of three buildings – a Taoist temple in the centre, a smaller Buddhist temple to the right, and living quarters for religious functionaries to the left. Inside the main Taoist shrine stands an altar to Tu Uyen, with the Immortal in the middle flanked by statues of his wife and son.

From Van Mieu head east along Nguyen Thai Hoc, turn south down Duong Le Duan and take the third turning to the east along busy Pho Tran Hung Dao. You are now entering the commercial heart of Downtown Hanoi, most of which was built by the French and which is now grad-

Altar to Confucius in the Great House of Ceremonies

Altar at Dao Quan Bich Cau

ually going high-rise. One small pagoda of distinction survives in this bustling business area, however – take the second turning north along Pho Trang Hung Dao and, at 73 Quan Su Street, you will find **Chua Quan Su** ⓯ or 'The Ambassadors Pagoda'. Little of the original 17th-century structure survives – the pagoda in its current form dates mainly from 1930. Once a reception house for ambassadors from Buddhist countries (representatives of other nations enjoying less favoured status were kept at a suitable distance from the seat of government), today it is an active and popular Buddhist establishment.

From Chua Quan Su head north a short distance to cross Pho Ly Thuong Kiet, turn eastwards and take the first road on the left along Pho Hoa Loa. On the west side of this small cross street stands all that remains of the **Maison Centrale**, the much-feared prison built by the French in 1896, where thousands of Vietnamese political prisoners were held during the colonial period. Today it is better known to Western visitors as **The Hanoi Hilton** ⓰ – a wry sobriquet given by US prisoners of war held here during the Second Indochina War. In recent years the greater part of the old prison has been torn down to make way for a glittering high-rise tower and little but the ochre-coloured main entrance and a small museum remains of the original building.

The Hanoi Hilton

From the Maison Centrale head north across Pho Hai Ba Trung to Pho Trang Thi and continue east past the southern shore of Hoa Hoan Kiem. This is the busy heart of Downtown Hanoi, and a good place both to eat and shop. If you have the time and energy it is worth making a small detour north along Ngo Quyen to see the former **Residence of the Governor of Tonkin**. Built in 1918 this very attractive colonial building now serves as a State Guest House for important visitors. The main attraction in this area, however, lies at the eastern end of Pho Trang Thi – the recently restored ★ **Opera House** ⓱, now known officially as the Municipal Theatre. This fine building, modelled on the neo-baroque Paris Opera, would be much admired in any major European capital. During colonial times the Opera House was regarded as the jewel in the crown of French Hanoi and the most sophisticated expression of French culture in all Indochina.

Residence of the Governor of Tonkin

To the east of the Opera House, near the Red River embankment, are a number of museums including the **Revolution Museum**, the **Geology Museum** and the **History Museum** ⓲ (Tuesday to Sunday 8.15–11.45am, 1.15–4.30pm). Founded in the 1930s by the prestigious Ecole Française d'Extrême Orient, this unusual building in Franco-Vietnamese style holds an interesting collection of artefacts from Vietnamese, Cham and Khmer history.

History Museum interior

Excursions from Hanoi

Cyclists at Co Loa

See map on page 32

There are a number of significant and interesting attractions in the immediate vicinity of Hanoi that are well worth visiting. Taken collectively, however, they do not constitute a single tour, being scattered at all points of the compass and varying distances from the Vietnamese capital. The best solution for those wishing to explore the area is to stay in the capital and travel by taxi or – where possible – bus to the various destinations, perhaps combining two or three in a single day if they are all in the same general direction.

The first known independent Viet kingdom was established in 258BC when Thuc Pan, Lord of Au Lac, overthrew the 18th and last ruler of the legendary Hung Kingdom, proclaimed himself King An Duong and established his capital at ★ **Co Loa**, 25km (16 miles) north of present day Hanoi. Today there is little left of the original city, but a half-day trip to Co Loa Citadel is worthwhile, both for the historical site itself and for an opportunity to see the attractive and relatively prosperous farming villages amidst which the Citadel is set.

King An Duong built his capital within three concentric ramparts which spiralled like the shell of a snail – Co Loa means 'Old Snail' – and they are still just discernible today. Close by the Citadel's former south gateway a venerable old bo tree shades **Den My Chau**, a temple dedicated to An Duong's daughter, the princess My Chau; inside is a headless stone statue said to represent the princess. About 100m (325ft) further on, **Den An Duong Vuong** is dedicated primarily to King An Duong, a 16th-century bronze statue of whom rests on the main altar,

Den My Chau temple

EXCURSIONS FROM HANOI & ROUTE 2

whilst a subsidiary altar is dedicated to the magical Golden Turtle Kim Quy. The terrace of this temple rests on six turned and lacquered pillars that support a long roof with gracefully upswept eaves.

The justly famous ★★ **Chua Huong** or Perfume Pagoda is set in the mountains some 60km (38 miles) south of Hanoi. Here you will find a number of Buddhist temples and shrines largely established by the Trinh Lords in the 17th and 18th centuries. It's possible to drive to Chua Huong, but the most enjoyable way to go is by boat from Duc Khe on the Yen River, a trip most easily organised through any tour company in Hanoi. The river trip through outstandingly beautiful countryside takes around two hours, after which it is necessary to walk about 4km (2½ miles) to the temple complex (about one and a half hours), so this should be considered a whole day trip.

Perfume Pagoda

Similarly well worth visiting is **Thay Pagoda**, about 40km (25 miles) southwest of Hanoi in Ha Tay Province. Thay or 'Master's' Pagoda, also known as **Thien Phuc Tu** or 'Heavenly Blessing' Pagoda, is dedicated to Thich Ca or Sakyamuni Buddha (the Buddha Gautama, born in 536BC). To the left of the main altar stands a statue of Tu Dao Hanh, the master after whom the pagoda is named. To the right stands a statue of King Ly Nhan Tong (1072–1127), who is held to have been a reincarnation of Tu Dao Hanh and during whose reign the pagoda was founded. Thay Pagoda contains more than 100 religious statues, including purportedly the two largest in Vietnam – clay and papier-mâché giants which weigh more than a 1,000kg (16 stone) each. Tu Dao Hanh is said to have been a master water puppeteer, and demonstrations of this ancient skill are given at the temple during the annual festival which takes place on the 5th to 7th days of the third lunar month. **Tay Phuong Pagoda** lies some 6km (4 miles) to the west – hence its name, which means 'Western Pagoda'. Perched on top of a hill said to resemble a buffalo, Tay Phuong is a small temple dating originally from the 8th century, which is notable for its collection of more than 70 fine jack-fruit wood statues, including figures from both the Buddhist and Confucian pantheons.

Thay Pagoda

The Red River Delta is well known for the skills of its artisans, and several small villages within easy reach of Hanoi are traditionally associated with particular crafts. About 13km (8 miles) southeast of the capital on the left bank of the Red River, the settlement of ★ **Bat Trang** is renowned for its blue and white ceramics – a tradition thought to date back to the 15th century when Muslim traders first introduced cobalt. There are approximately

2,000 families in Bat Trang, managing more than 800 kilns. The speciality of the 30 or so acknowledged 'master potters' is reproduction antiques. Other craft villages in the Hanoi region include **Van Phuc**, about 8km (5 miles) southwest of the capital on Highway 6 to Hoa Binh, famous for its silk production; **So**, a noodle-producing village about 12km (7½ miles) further out on the same road; and **Dong Ky**, a wood carving village about 15km (9 miles) northeast of the capital on Highway 1 to Bac Ninh. Visitors are most welcome at all these craft villages, and most tour companies in Hanoi are able to arrange half- or one day tours.

If you are flying out of Hanoi's Noi Bai Airport and need to kill a little time in the vicinity, consider visiting **Chua Soc Son**, a temple dedicated to Thanh Giong, a legendary hero who defeated the Chinese during the time of the Hung Kings. The temple, set beside a tranquil lake against pine-clad hills, is about 35km (22 miles) to the north of the capital, on Highway 3 to Dong Anh, just north of Noi Bai. **But Thap Pagoda** is another quiet and seldom-visited temple, which dates from the 17th century and is on the south bank of the Duong River, about 25km (16 miles) east of Hanoi to the south of Bach Ninh. There are several other temples in the vicinity, notably **Van Phuc Pagoda** – your taxi-driver or tour agent will know the way.

Outcrops at Hoa Lu

Finally mention should be made of two important attractions somewhat further afield. ★ **Hoa Lu** was the ancient capital of Vietnam under the Dinh (968–80) and Early Le (980–1009) Dynasties. Set amidst spectacular karst outcrops in central Ninh Binh Province, some 94km (58 miles) south of Hanoi, are two historic temples. The first, **Dinh Tien Hoang**, was restored in the 17th century and is dedicated to the Dinh Kings. Inside are statues of Emperor Dinh Tien Hoang and three of his sons. The second, **Dai Hanh**, is similarly dedicated to the memory of the Early Le Kings.

The town of **Thai Nguyen**, 76km (48 miles) northeast of Hanoi, is unremarkable apart from the exceptionally good **Museum of the Nationalities of Vietnam** (Tuesday, Wednesday and Sunday 8–11am, 2–4pm). If you are interested in Vietnam's complex ethnic mosaic, and especially in the hill peoples, a visit to the museum is well worth the journey. The exhibits, which include everyday artefacts, costumes, photographs and video presentations, are displayed in five sizeable rooms divided by linguistic category. The Mon-Khmer Room, recently redesigned with Swedish expertise and financial assistance, is particularly noteworthy. The museum, a large pink-coloured building, stands by a roundabout in the centre of town.

Route 2

Halong Bay

Haiphong and Halong Bay

Haiphong – Du Hang Pagoda – Do Son Beach – Hong Gai – Halong City – Halong Bay – Cat Ba National Park *See map on page 32*

The great flood plain of the Red River Delta stretches east from Hanoi to Haiphong and the sea. Here, amidst the coves and inlets of the Gulf of Tonkin, lies one of the natural wonders of Southeast Asia, even of the world. Both Vietnamese and overseas visitors are flocking to this region in increasing numbers as facilities improve – for the seafood, swimming and sunbathing, to be sure – but above all to marvel at the magnificence of Halong Bay.

To reach Halong Bay head east along Highway 5 for just over 100km (63 miles) to reach **Haiphong**, Vietnam's major port and fourth largest city. An important industrial centre, Haiphong's strategic significance meant that it attracted heavy American bombardment during the Second Indochina War. The suburbs suffered particularly badly and – shoddily rebuilt and dominated by a huge, pollution-belching cement works – are not compelling. The town centre is much more pleasant, with a number of broad boulevards flanked by shady flame trees and several attractive colonial buildings, notably the wine-coloured **Haiphong Museum** on Dien Bien Phuc Street, the salmon-pink **Theatre** on Hoang Van Thu, and the 19th-century **Cathedral** by the Tam Bac River.

If you are staying in town, the 17th-century **Du Hang Pagoda** located on Pho Chua Hang to the south of the railway tracks is worth a visit for its elaborate architecture and tranquil aspect. Close by on Nguyen Cong Tru Street

Downtown Haiphong

stands **Dinh Hang Kenh**, a traditional communal house raised on ironwood columns facing an ornamental lake.

About 20km (12 miles) southeast of Haiphong, at the end of a hilly promontory jutting into the sea, the town of Do Son is popular with Vietnamese day-trippers but lacks any real appeal – except, that is, to visitors from nearby China, who seemingly cannot resist the siren-call of Vietnam's first casino. Palm-lined **Do Son Beach**, however, overlooking a group of islets in the Gulf of Tonkin, is fine for a swim if you are staying in the Haiphong area.

But most travellers will prefer to continue towards Halong Bay, either by road or – a slower but more interesting option – by boat. Ferries leave Haiphong at 6 and 11am, taking about three hours to reach **Hong Gai**, Halong's main port. There are no special attractions to be found here – the dockside is dilapidated and grubby with dust from decades of coal shipments – but to the south of the ferry pier, in the lee of a limestone outcrop named **Nui Bai Tho** or 'Poem Mountain', is a picturesque fishing village. If you have time, it is interesting to stroll through the village noting the poems in praise of the beauty of Halong Bay which have been carved into the rocky face of Nui Bai Tho over the centuries.

From Hong Gai it is just a short ferry ride across the narrow Cua Luc Channel to the town of **Bai Chay**, conjoined with Hong Gai since 1994 to create **Halong City**. Where Hong Gai is grimy and industrial, Bai Chay is northern Vietnam's most developed resort. Designed to appeal primarily to locals and to visitors from nearby China, karaoke bars and neon lights abound, but this slightly sleazy aspect in no way detracts from the beauty of the emerald sea and gem-like garland of the islands spread to the south.

Paradise found

In Vietnamese *ha long* means 'descending dragon', and legend has it that ★★★ **Halong Bay** was formed by a gigantic dragon which plunged into the Gulf of Tonkin, creating thousands of limestone outcrops by the lashing of its tail. Geologists tend to dismiss this theory, arguing that the myriad islands that dot Halong Bay and extend all the way north to the Chinese frontier are the product of selective erosion of the seabed over millennia.

Either way, the result is outstandingly beautiful. More than 2,000 cragged, pinnacle-shaped islets are scattered across 1,500sq km (580sq miles) of bay, making an excursion by boat a memorable experience – not least for the eerie experience of sailing through silent, sea-girt caves. Boats can be chartered locally in either Bai Chay or around the harbour in Hong Gai; alternatively almost any travel agent in Halong City or Hanoi will be only too pleased to arrange matters. The most spectacular islands and dramatic caves lie in the west part of the bay – your boatman will certainly be acquainted with all the best sights. A full day tour of the islands is advised, though shorter trips are possible – lunch or dinner on board, generally fresh seafood, is highly recommended, but should be arranged beforehand.

All aboard

An alternative way to see Halong Bay is via **Cat Ba Island** which also permits a visit to **Cat Ba National Park**. The easiest way to get to the island is by air-conditioned express boat from Haiphong (9am daily except Tuesday), although there are also two slow ferries each day. The route to Cat Ba cuts across the estuary of the **Bach Dang River** where the Vietnamese routed invading Chinese forces in 938AD and destroyed an attacking Mongol fleet in 1288. Boats dock at Cat Ba Town, the only settlement of any size, where it is possible to overnight and eat in some comfort. From Cat Ba Town it is a simple matter to visit **Cat Ba National Park** and explore its rugged, pristine scenery. The park, which is chiefly known for its population of rare golden-headed langurs, is also home to an astonishing range of flora – more than 750 species of plants have been identified to date.

Boats may readily be chartered to explore Halong Bay to the north, or the smaller but picturesque **Lan Ha Bay** to the northeast of Cat Ba Town. It's also possible to reach Halong City by boat from Cat Ba, making a crossing of Halong Bay en route.

Spectacular islands and dramatic caves

Beyond Halong Bay the remarkable limestone outcrops continue to stud the sea northwards to the Chinese frontier by way of **Ba Tu Long Bay**. A charter to this scenic area, as yet all but unvisited by tourists, can be arranged from Halong City and takes about five hours each way.

Route 3

Sapa and Dien Bien Phu

Song Hong – Lao Cai – Sapa – Lai Chau – Dien Bien Phu – Son La – Hoa Binh *See map on page 39*

Mountainous northwestern Vietnam offers some of the most spectacular scenery in the country, as well as the opportunity to visit minority hill peoples who still preserve their unique cultural identities and speak languages other than Vietnamese. It's also home to the secluded valley of Dien Bien Phu, close to the watershed with Laos, where the most decisive battle of Vietnam's long struggle against French imperialism was fought and won. A high point, literally, is the ascent of Vietnam's highest mountain, Fansipan. The northwest is not an easy part of the country to travel in, however. The loop described below takes about a week to complete. Roads are poor and sometimes induce vertigo, so a 4WD vehicle or powerful motorbike is essential for independent travel beyond Lao Cai.

En route to Lao Cai

The most interesting way to reach the northwest is via the single line metre gauge track to Lao Cai on the Chinese frontier. Inaugurated in 1910, the track continues to Kunming, the capital of China's Yunnan Province, linking with the Chinese rail system. Trains for Lao Cai leave Hanoi daily at 9.45pm, but it is more rewarding to take the 5.10am, arriving at Lao Cai at 3.35pm, in plenty of time to find a hotel and look around town. This schedule also permits you to see some spectacular scenery, as the track follows the narrow **Song Hong** or **Red River Valley**. The French, who supervised the construction of the Hanoi-Kunming Railway, hoped it would become a major trade route between Vietnam and China. The reality fell short of their expectations, but the line – though dilapidated – remains a remarkable piece of engineering.

Traffic on the Red River

There is little of interest in **Lao Cai**, which is really just a place to have a meal and spend the night before heading on into the hills. There are no historic buildings or monuments, the Chinese having razed the entire town in 1979 during the Third Indochina War. Following the Chinese withdrawal, the border remained firmly closed until 1993, but today Chinese tourists and traders are everywhere to be seen. It's interesting in the late afternoon to walk to the Chinese border crossing and watch the constant stream of humanity crossing the narrow **Coc Leu Bridge**.

The hill town of ★ **Sapa** is just 38km (24 miles) from Lao Cai by way of a winding, metalled road which climbs slowly into the hills. Developed in 1922 as a hill station – those universal retreats constructed by European colonial administrations all over the east to escape from the heat and humidity of the plains – Sapa lies in an attractive valley at an elevation of 1600m (5,200ft) and is pleasantly cool during the hot season. Should you visit during the winter months, however, bring warm clothing, as rain and drizzle are prevalent and temperatures regularly fall to freezing point at night. Whilst a visit to Sapa makes a refreshing change from the plains at any time of year, the best months are September–November and March–May. Besides the beautiful scenery and cool climate, this small market town affords the visitor a chance to enjoy temperate fruits such as plums, peaches and apples, as well as to meet with the local hill peoples, among whom the most numerous are the colourfully dressed Hmong and Dao.

Most people living in Sapa town are ethnic Viets, while the Hmong and Dao tend to live in small villages in the vicinity. It's possible to walk to these settlements – the Hmong village of Cat Cat, just 3km (2 miles) distant, is a popular choice, and there are Dao, Red Dao and Tay villages within a circumference of about 12km (7½ miles) – but most people plan their visit to coincide with the popular ★ **Weekend Market**. This event, which is of social as well as commercial significance to the local hill peoples, is well worth seeing. Every week, from noon on

Weekend Market at Sapa

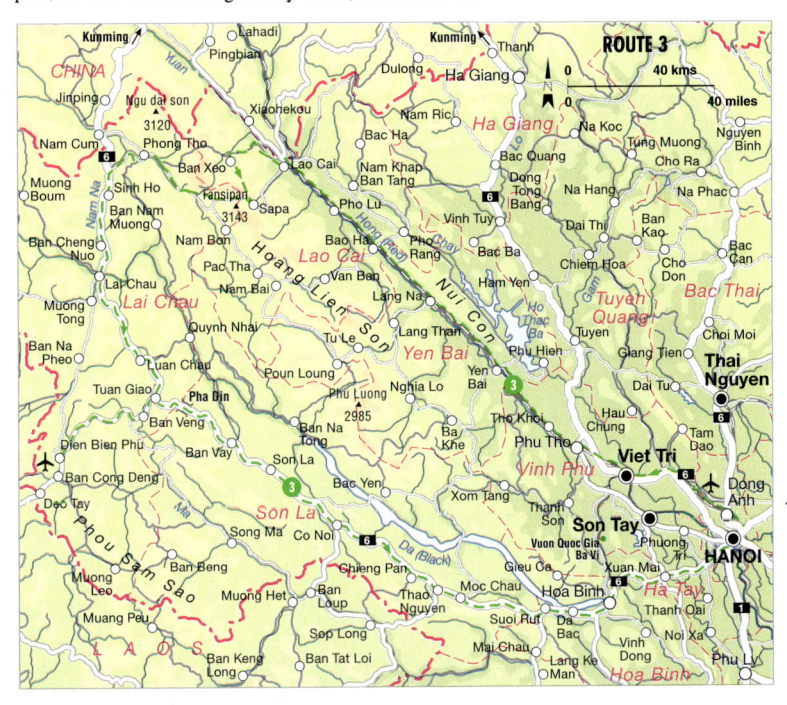

On the way to market

Saturday to noon on Sunday, people flock into Sapa from the surrounding villages to trade (increasingly bringing hill tribe artefacts for sale to foreigners), gossip and look for potential marriage partners. The women, especially, dress in their finest clothing, sporting leggings, embroidered skirts and jackets, heavy silver jewellery and – most notably the Red Dao women – elaborate headdresses.

If you are fit and healthy, then a rewarding excursion from Sapa is the ascent of **Fansipan**, at 3,143m (10,215ft) the highest mountain in the surrounding Hoang Lien Range, and also in all Vietnam. Fansipan is only 10km (6 miles) from Sapa, but the terrain is difficult and the weather frequently bad – warm clothes, good boots, camping equipment and a guide are essential, as the round trip may take up to 5 days. You will also need to carry supplies, so it is best to make arrangements through a local trekking agency. For most of the climb, the countryside is completely bereft of signs of humanity, just forest, monkeys, birds and fine mountain views.

Beyond Sapa the road deteriorates as it rises to cross the 1,900m (6,200ft) **Tram Ton Pass**. It's 180km (112 miles) and 8 hours to the remote but beautifully located town of **Lai Chau**, along treacherous roads that offer spellbinding vistas. There's nothing much to do in Lai Chau, though it's a convenient place to stay overnight, with a reasonable hotel and good restaurant. In the morning it's another 110km (69 miles) or 4 hours to ★ **Dien Bien Phu**, a remote settlement just 15km (9 miles) from the Lao frontier. Today the Muong Thanh Valley that surrounds Dien Bien Phu is calm and peaceful, but it wasn't always thus. In 1954 Vietnam's most celebrated military commander, General Vo Nguyen Giap, successfully besieged and then reduced the French garrison occupying the valley. More than 13,000 soldiers were killed or taken prisoner, destroying the French will to fight and effectively bringing the First Indochina War to an end. Today the old battlefield has become a tourist attraction. The former HQ of the French commander, Colonel de Castries, has been rebuilt and some rusting French tanks and heavy artillery pieces are collected nearby.

Memorial at Dien Bien Phu

The return journey to Hanoi takes about 18 hours by road. Most people choose to break their journey and overnight in the provincial capital of **Son La**, around 150km (94 miles) and 8 hours east of Dien Bien Phu on Highway 6. From here it's a further 320km (200 miles) or about 10 hours to Hanoi via **Hoa Binh**. The scenery en route is pleasant, but not exceptional, so many people will prefer the quicker and easier option of flying from Dien Bien Phu to Hanoi – at present there are three flights a week.

Detail of Khai Dinh's mausoleum, Hue

Route 4

Hue and Environs

See map on page 43

The former imperial city of ★★★ **Hue** is the most important historical and cultural monument in Vietnam. It is also a place of great beauty, despite having been badly damaged during the 1968 Tet Offensive. Renowned throughout the country both for the beauty of its women and for the sophistication of its cuisine, Hue lies at the heart of Vietnamese cultural tradition. The beautiful Song Huong or Perfume River flows through the centre of the city, whilst the surrounding countryside is studded with elaborate tombs built during the time of the Nguyen Emperors. For the visitor there is only one possible problem – the weather at Hue is notoriously unpredictable, and rainfall is frequent.

Visitors to Hue, whether travelling by air, rail or road, generally enter the city from the southwest, via the newer commercial quarter which dates from the colonial period. It is here that the greatest selection of hotels, restaurants and bars may be found. Imperial Hue, demarcated by the crenellated walls of its great Citadel, lies on the far side of the Perfume River, a monument to past imperial glory and more recent desperate events.

Dominating the skyline is the 37-m (120-ft) high ★ **Cot Co** or **Flag Tower** ❶, erected in 1809. Cot Co achieved international renown on the morning of 31 January 1968, when communist forces seized the Citadel and ran their yellow-starred banner up its tall mast. For the following 25 days the Viet Cong flag fluttered defiantly as US Marines and South Vietnamese soldiers fought house-

Inhabitant of Hue

Hue's renowned Flag Tower

to-house to retake the city. During this brutal struggle Hue was battered by machine guns, rockets, bombs, napalm, artillery fire and naval bombardment, causing immense destruction. Further damage ensued following the collapse of the south, as symbols of Vietnam's royal past were left to decay by the victorious communists – a policy which changed sharply in 1990, as the potential for tourism was realised. In 1993 UNESCO declared Hue a World Heritage Site. Restoration and conservation work continue.

Hue children

Originally part of the Kingdom of Champa, Hue first became part of Vietnam in 1306 when King Jaya Sinhavarman III capriciously renounced all Cham territories north of the Hai Van Pass in exchange for the hand of Huyen Tran, a beautiful Vietnamese princess. In 1558 Hue – then known as Phu Xuan – became capital of the Nguyen Lords of the south. In 1802 Nguyen Anh, the last of the Nguyen Lords, defeated his northern rivals and proclaimed the city capital of a reunited Vietnam, changing its name to Hue and his own to Gia Long, first of the Nguyen Emperors.

Three years later Gia Long ordered the construction of ★★ **Kinh Thanh**, Hue's moated Citadel. This vast structure is an unusual hybrid, built according to the notions of Chinese geomancy, but in the style of the noted French military architect Sebastien de Vauban. Thus the complex is oriented southeast towards Nui Ngu Binh, or 'Royal Screen Mountain' – a low hill believed to deflect harmful influences from the Nguyen capital. To reinforce this auspicious aspect of its location, massive brick walls about 6m (20ft) high, 20m (65ft) thick and almost 10km (6 miles) long protect the Citadel. These walls are ringed by lotus-filled moats and punctuated by towers, with crenellated ramparts, an earth glacis and no fewer than 24 Vauban-inspired bastions.

Access to the Citadel is by way of 10 fortified gates, each of which is reached by a low, slightly arched stone bridge across the moat. In imperial times a cannon would sound at 5am and 9pm to mark the opening and closing of the gates. The area within the Citadel – in all, 520 hectares (1300 acres) – comprises three concentric enclosures, the first of which was formerly used to accommodate the Imperial Ministries and which now constitutes a pleasant area of parks, gardens and quiet residential districts. Here may be found the **Nine Holy Cannons**, kept in buildings flanking the gates on either side of the Flag Tower. The massive but symbolic weapons were cast on the order of Gia Long to protect his new capital. Made from bronze that was captured from the defeated Tay Son army, the nine cannons are said to represent the Four Seasons and the Five Elements – namely earth, metal, wood, water and fire.

A second moat and defensive wall within the Citadel guard the ★★ **Hoang Thanh** or **Yellow Imperial City** ❷, modelled by Gia Long on the Forbidden City in Beijing. This inner city, generally referred to as *Dai Noi* or 'Great Enclosure', has four gates, the chief of which – in direct alignment with the Flag Tower to the southeast – is called ★ **Cua Ngo Mon** or 'Meridian Gate'. This majestic entrance, constructed by Emperor Minh Mang in 1833, is considered amongst the finest surviving examples of Nguyen architecture. There are five entrances – the central way, reserved for the emperor alone, is flanked by lesser openings for mandarins and court officials; these in turn are flanked by two much larger entrances for the royal elephants. Above the massive stone slabs of the main gateway rests **Five Phoenix Watchtower** where the emperor sat enthroned on state occasions. Above this pavilion is

Cua Ngo Mon

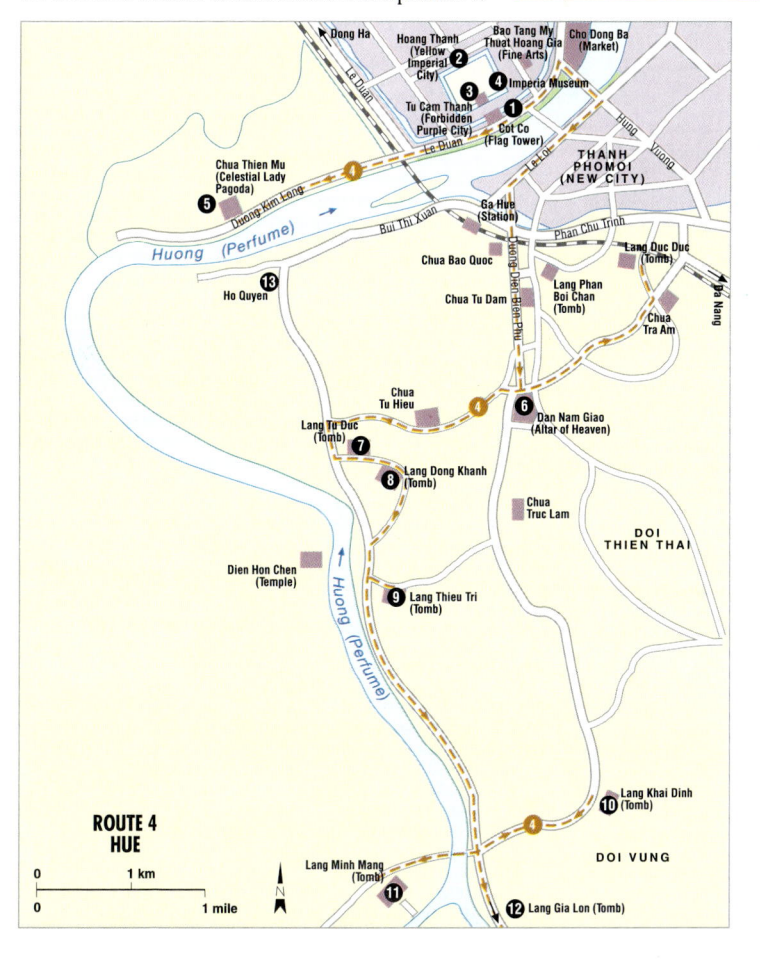

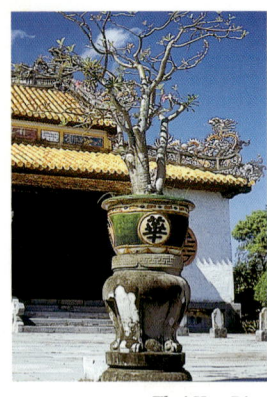

a small room reached by a concealed staircase where ladies of the royal court could see through finely-carved grilles without being observed.

Beyond the Ngo Mon Gate **Kim Thuy Kieu**, the 'Bridge of Golden Waters', which only the emperor was permitted to cross, leads between two tranquil, lotus-filled ponds to ★★ **Thai Hoa Dien**, the 'Hall of Supreme Harmony'. This palace, the throne room of the Nguyen Kings, is the most splendid of Hue's surviving palaces. Originally built by Gia Long in 1805, it escaped serious damage during the Tet Offensive but was in an advanced state of decay until restoration work started in 1991. The yellow-tiled roof is supported by 80 massive wooden columns lacquered a deep red and decorated with golden dragons, the emblem of the Nguyen Dynasty.

Thai Hoa Dien

Ceremonial urn next to Dai Cung Mon

Behind the throne room **Dai Cung Mon** or 'Great Golden Gate' permits access to the **Tu Cam Thanh** or **Forbidden Purple City** ❸, formerly the sole preserve of the emperor, his queen, nine separate ranks of concubines, and female palace servants. No man but the king could set foot in this 10 hectare (25 acre) city-within-a-city on pain of death – his own sons were banished when they reached puberty, and the only non-females allowed inside were palace eunuchs. In imperial times the Purple City consisted of more than 60 buildings arranged around 20 courtyards, but it was seriously damaged by fire in 1947, a tragedy compounded by the disastrous Tet Offensive. Fortunately photographs and detailed plans have survived, and restoration work is underway. Today much of the former Purple City is given over to vegetable gardens, though in the northeastern quarter the **Thai Binh Lau** or **Royal Library**, an elegant two-storey structure built during the reign of Minh Mang (1820–41), survives and has been restored.

Inside the Forbidden Purple City

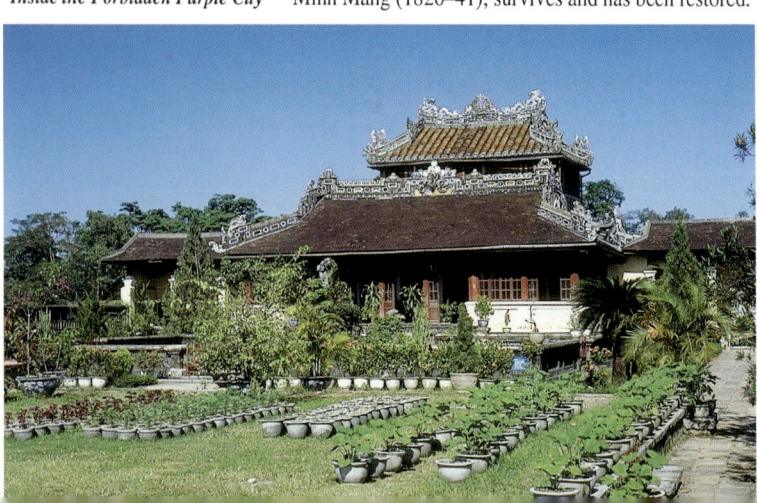

Before leaving the Citadel it is worth visiting ★ **The Mieu** or 'Temple of the Generations', dedicated to the Nguyen Emperors who built Hue. Located in the southwest of the Imperial City and currently under restoration, the temple houses 10 funerary tablets honouring Nguyen rulers from Gia Long to Khai Dinh (1802–1925). In the courtyard facing The Mieu stand nine large bronze vessels. These are the famous ★ **Cuu Dinh** or **Dynastic Urns** of the Nguyen Dynasty. Cast on the orders of Emperor Minh Mang in 1835, they weigh about two tons each. Decorated with elegant bas-reliefs rich in symbolic detail – dragon, phoenix, elephant, tiger, sun, moon, stars – they played an important part in the cult of imperial ancestor worship.

Still within the Citadel but on Le Truc Street, just outside **Cua Hien Nhon**, the Imperial City's northeastern gate, the ★ **Imperial Museum** ❹ is well worth visiting. Housed in the **Long An Palace**, a fine old building dating back to 1845, the walls are inscribed with poetry written in *chu nom* or 'Southern Writing', a demotic script employing modified Chinese characters which was developed in the 15th century and, by Nguyen times, had become the chief vehicle for vernacular Vietnamese literature. The exhibits consist chiefly of royal paraphernalia and assorted gifts from past emperors.

Detail of a Dynastic Urn

Beyond the Citadel Hue has numerous widely scattered attractions. To the northeast of the citadel is a large, triangular island lying between Dong Ba Canal and the Perfume River. Here, in the busy, congested streets of **Phu Cat**, the former Merchants' Quarter, much of Hue's commerce is still carried on. At 120 Chi Lang Street, deep in this quarter, may be found the small **mosque** which once served Hue's Tamil Muslims, business people originally hailing from the French colony of Pondicherry in south India. Unhappy at the strictures of a socialist economy, Hue's Muslims have long since departed, but the mosque remains and today functions as a private house.

On the north bank of the Perfume River, about 4km (2½ miles) southwest of the Citadel, stands the famous ★★ **Thien Mu Pagoda** ❺, long considered a symbol for the City of Hue. Originally founded in 1601 by Lord Nguyen Hoang, the most striking feature of the temple is a 21-m (68-ft) high octagonal tower, the seven-storey **Thap Phuoc Duyen** or 'Tower of the Source of Happiness', which stands atop a small hillock overlooking the Perfume River. Two pavilions close by house, respectively, a stone stele erected in 1715 which records the history of Buddhism in Hue, and a large bronze bell, cast in 1710, which weighs over 2,000 kg (70 stone). The sound of this bell is said to reach over 10km (6 miles), and in times

Thien Mu Pagoda

past could clearly be heard in the Citadel and throughout the surrounding villages. As an ancient poem has it:

> *The breeze cradles the swaying stems of bamboo*
> *The Thien Mu Bell rings out*
> *And the crowing cockerels of Tho Xuong*
>   *village respond...*

If Thien Mu is considered the religious heart of Buddhism in Hue, then **Van Mieu**, the **Temple of Literature**, holds the same status for Confucianism. Founded by Gia Long in 1808, the temple, situated on the north bank of the Perfume River about 1km (½ mile) west of Thien Mu, was intended by the Nguyen Emperor to replace the long-established Temple of Literature in Hanoi. In fact Hue's Van Mieu is a much less imposing structure than the capital's venerable complex, but it is still worth a visit, both for the views of the nearby Perfume River and to see the inscribed doctoral stelae of the Nguyen Emperors.

On the south bank of the Perfume River, beyond the former French quarter now known as Khu Pho Moi or 'New City' is **Nam Giao Dan** or the **Altar of Heaven** ❻. During the years of Hue's primacy this was the most important religious site in the country, though today there isn't a lot to see beyond a series of three raised terraces. The first, square terrace represents man, the second, also square, represents earth, whilst the topmost, round terrace represents heaven. Here, approximately every three years between 1806 and 1945, the Nguyen Emperors reaffirmed the legitimacy of their rule through a series of elaborate sacrifices to the Emperor of Heaven.

Scattered across the countryside to the south and west of the city, the ★★★ **Tombs of the Nguyen Emperors** are, together with the Citadel, Hue's greatest attraction. Although 13 rulers sat on the imperial throne between 1802 and 1945, only seven were given the honour of their own royal mausoleum. The seven tombs, all of which have features of outstanding architectural merit, are often strikingly different. They can be reached by bicycle or motorbike – both readily available for hire in Hue – and make at least two rewarding day trips.

The Vietnamese word for tomb is *lang*, and this is used as a standard prefix for all the royal tombs. **Lang Duc Duc** (pronounced 'Zuc Duc') is the tomb nearest to Hue, but also one of the hardest to find. Located just south of the railway line on Tan Lang Lane, it was constructed as recently as 1899 but had fallen into a bad state of disrepair and is currently undergoing restoration. Duc Duc, the nephew and adopted son of Tu Duc, reigned for a mere three days in 1883. Dethroned as a result of court intrigue,

Plying the Perfume River

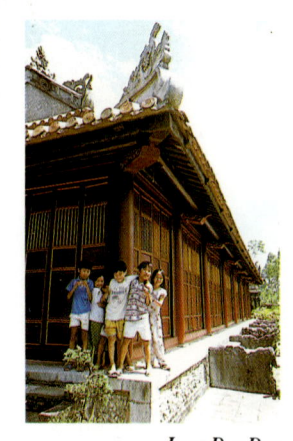

Lang Duc Duc

he later starved to death in prison. According to legend, he was being taken to a common burial when the mat in which he was being carried split open, so he was summarily buried on the spot.

Six years later, in a twist of fate, his son Thanh Thai (1889–1907) became emperor and erected a mausoleum for Duc Duc over the spot where he had been buried. While Duc Duc is considered to have been sympathetic to the French, his son Thanh Thai and grandson Duy Tan were opposed to colonial rule and are considered 'patriotic kings' by the ruling communists. Thanh Thai was deposed by the French in 1907, as was Duy Than in 1916. Both father and son were exiled to Réunion. Thanh Thai returned in 1953, died in Vung Tau a year later and was buried in his father's tomb the same year. The remains of Duy Tan, who was killed in a plane crash in Africa while fighting for the allies in World War II, were brought back to Vietnam after the communist victory and finally interred in the family mausoleum in 1987.

About 6km (4 miles) southwest of Hue, set amidst pine-covered hills in Thuy Xuan district, is the splendid mausoleum of Emperor Tu Duc (1848–83). ★★★ **Lang Tu Duc** ❼, built between 1864 and 1867, is perhaps the most exquisitely designed of the Nguyen mausoleums. It's built on a grand scale, but with a perfect eye for detail. Designed by Tu Duc himself, the mausoleum is set amidst fragrant pines and frangipani trees, surrounded by tranquil, lotus-filled waters. It was Tu Duc's habit to recline here in the gorgeous Xung Khiem Pavilion composing poetry and reflecting – one might suspect – on the transience of mundane existence. A lovely place indeed, but not without its dark side. When Tu Duc expired he was buried secretly, reputedly with great treasure. Reportedly all 200 of the servants involved in the burial were subsequently beheaded to keep the emperor's final resting-place hidden from tomb robbers and safe from desecration!

An unsealed road leads southeast from Lang Tu Duc to ★ **Lang Dong Khanh** ❽, the mausoleum of Emperor Dong Khanh (1885–8). Like Duc Duc, Dong Khanh was the nephew and adopted son of the childless Tu Duc. His mausoleum, the smallest of the Nguyen Tombs, is unusually well preserved. The exterior of the main temple is elaborate and delicate. The interior shows signs of French cultural influence already impinging on Nguyen tastes – look in particular for the engravings of Napoleon and the Battle of Waterloo which hang from the red-lacquered ironwood pillars supporting the roof.

Head southwards along the Perfume River about 1½km (1 mile) from Lang Tu Duc before turning east for a short distance to find ★ **Lang Thieu Tri** ❾, the mausoleum

Aspects of Lang Tu Duc

Lang Dong Khan

of Emperor Thieu Tri (1841–47). One of the smaller tombs, it lacks the usual walled gardens and is divided into two sections. To the west is the actual tomb, whilst to the east is a finely executed temple set among small lakes.

To reach ★★ **Lang Khai Dinh** ⑩, the mausoleum of Emperor Khai Dinh (1916–25), head south along Dien Bien Phu Road to Dan Nam Giao Road, then continue south along Minh Mang Road. It's about 10km (6 miles) to the extraordinary architectural melange which marks Khai Dinh's final resting-place. Built between 1920 and 1931, the tomb rises through a series of stairs and courtyards on the side of a low hill. The architect clearly sought to combine Vietnamese and French cultural traditions in this tomb, and the result is not altogether unsuccessful.

Perhaps the most impressive of all the Nguyen Tombs, ★★★ **Lang Minh Mang** ⑪, the mausoleum of Emperor Minh Mang (1820–41), is located on the left bank of the Perfume River about 12km (7½ miles) from Hue. Planned in Minh Mang's lifetime but executed after his death, the complex – which includes elegant portals, bridges, lakes and pavilions, as well as the Sung An Temple dedicated to the Emperor and Empress – blends harmoniously with the surrounding countryside.

The last of the Nguyen Tombs, **Lang Gia Long** ⑫, mausoleum of the first Nguyen Emperor Gia Long (1802–20), is also located on the left bank of the Perfume River, a 20-minute boat ride and subsequent short walk south of the Minh Mang ferry crossing. Remote from Hue and badly damaged during the Second Indochina War, relatively few people visit this tomb.

Lang Minh Mang

Ho Quyen arena

If time permits, an interesting side trip may be made to **Ho Quyen**, the **Royal Arena** of the Nguyen Emperors, located 4km (2½ miles) southwest of Hue near the village of Phuong Duc. In times past tigers, were forced to fight elephants in this amphitheatre, and the elephant – seen as a symbol of imperial power – was expected to win. Consequently the contests were rather one-sided, with the unfortunate tiger having its claws removed and its mouth sewn shut before it entered the ring. Fortunately the last fight was held in 1904.

No visit to Hue is complete without a boat trip on the ★★ **Perfume River**. Boats are available for hire, either for an exploratory trip in the vicinity of Hue, or for a longer journey upstream to the tombs of Minh Mang and Gia Long. It's hard to explain the uncanny beauty of the river, though doubtless the iridescent, aquamarine waters, together with the profusion of colourful craft and boat women sporting *non la* – the ubiquitous cream-coloured conical hat of Vietnam – all contribute to the effect. On a clear, sunny day the Perfume River can indeed be magical.

View near Da Nang

Route 5

Hue to Da Nang and Hoi An

Hue – Canh Duong Beach – Hai Van Pass – Da Nang – Hoi An *See map on page 50*

Da Nang, Vietnam's fourth largest city, has ample accommodation and good seafood restaurants, but – with the notable exception of its remarkable Cham Museum – lacks intrinsic interest and is primarily useful as a base for visiting nearby attractions. Hoi An, by contrast, is quite exceptional, being beyond question the most attractive coastal town in all Vietnam, packed with sites of historical interest and noted for the excellence of its cuisine.

It takes about three hours to travel from Hue to Da Nang, and in good weather the drive is outstandingly beautiful. For the first 50km (31 miles) the Highway 1 parallels Thuy Tu and Cau Hai lagoons, both home to tens of thousands of seabirds. The road then climbs over a low range of hills before meeting the sea at Lang Co Village and palm-fringed Canh Duong Beach. There is good swimming here, and if you are making the trip to Da Nang into a day's excursion, this is the place to stop for lunch.

Cham Museum in Da Nang

Beyond Lang Co the road climbs steeply to snake across a spur of the Annamese Cordillera that juts into the South China Sea. This is the famous ★★ **Deo Hai Van** or 'Pass of the Ocean Clouds', so called because the 500-m (1,600-ft) high pass is often swathed in clouds and mist. When the weather's clear, the views are fantastic – but when enveloped in cloud, watch out for the small boulders left in the middle of the road by drivers who use them as chocks for their trucks! Until 1306 Hai Van formed the frontier between Vietnam and Champa, and the pass remains

50

strategically significant down to the present day. The summit is marked by an old French fort which appears fleetingly through the swirling mist.

The city of **Da Nang**, on the southern side of Hai Van, marks the northern limits of Vietnam's tropical zone and enjoys winters that are markedly warmer than in nearby Hue. Seized by the French in 1859, Da Nang rapidly developed into the main port of central Vietnam – a status reinforced during the Second Indochina War, when it became a massive base for the United States Air Force. Despite the size of the city, the ★★ **Cham Museum** or **Bao Tang Cham** is really the only major attraction. Located near the bank of the Han River in the southernmost part of the town centre, the museum was founded in 1915 by the prestigious Ecole Française d'Extrême Orient and ingeniously designed to provide an open-air setting, which protected the artefacts from bad weather and theft. Unfortunately the latter aim has not been entirely successful – several unique pieces have disappeared from the covered museum galleries in recent years.

Downtown Da Nang

The museum literally overflows with wonderful sandstone carvings from the Kingdom of Champa dating from the 7th to the 15th centuries. Figures from the pantheon of Hindu deities, notably Vishnu, Shiva, Uma, Ganesh and Nandi are a recurrent theme, as indeed is the female breast, an important icon of Cham religious art. Perhaps most famous of all the carvings is the exquisite dancing *apsara* of Tra Kieu on display in the northwest corner of Gallery Three. If you visit only one museum in Vietnam, this should be it.

Sights in the vicinity of Da Nang include **Marble Mountains**, about 7km (4 miles) southeast of the city, and **China Beach** in the same area. The former contain numerous caverns which used to serve as a Viet Cong guerrilla base and which have long housed a series of shrines dedicated to Buddha or to Confucius. The latter – in fact a line of beaches stretching almost 30km (18 miles) south of Da Nang – was a favourite 'Rest and Recreation' area for US servicemen during the Second Indochina War.

Sculpture at Marble Mountains

The small but historic town of ★★★ **Hoi An**, located on the Thu Bon River 30km (18 miles) south of Da Nang, holds far more appeal than its big northern neighbour. During the time of the Nguyen Lords and even under the first Nguyen Emperors, Hoi An – then known as Faifo – was an important port, visited regularly by shipping from Europe and all over the East. By the mid-19th century, however, the progressive silting up of the Thu Bon River and the development of nearby Da Nang combined to make Hoi An into a backwater, both literally and figuratively.

About town in Hoi An

Shrine on the Cau Nhat Ban

Street life

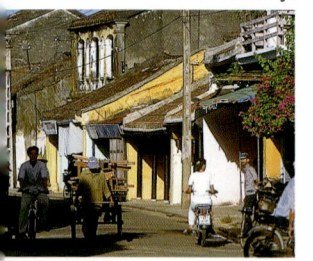

The result is a delightful old town with many of its historical monuments preserved – a place where the visitor may profitably linger and explore for several days.

Perhaps the best-known historical monument in town is ★ **Cau Nhat Ban** or the **Japanese Covered Bridge**. Originally built in 1593 by the Japanese mercantile community residing in Hoi An, this roofed, red-painted wooden bridge crosses a narrow side channel of the Thu Bon River in the western part of town. Tthough repeatedly restored, it retains its distinctly Japanese feel. A small temple, Chua Cau, is built into the northern side of the bridge.

Hoi An is famous for its ★★ **Traditional Houses**, most of which are found along Tran Phu, Nguyen Tai Hoc and Bach Dang Streets, in the vicinity of the waterfront. Although generally still inhabited, these old mercantile homes are open to visitors for the payment of a small fee. The best-known house is ★★ **Tan Ky House**, a fine example of an 18th-century Sino-Viet shophouse built around a tiny central courtyard. Look for the elegant 'crab shell' ceiling and the exquisite mother-of-pearl inlay Chinese poetry hanging from the columns supporting the roof. The nearby ★ **Phung Hung House** has been home to the same family for eight generations, traditionally traders in perfumed woods and spices from the nearby Central Highlands. Supported by no fewer than 80 hardwood columns, this building shows both Chinese influence (the gallery and shuttered windows) and Japanese influence (the delicate glass skylights). Finally, mention should be made of ★ **Diep Dong Nguyen House**, a 19th-century building, formerly a traditional Chinese pharmacy, which now has a fine collection of antique furniture and old photographs – these are family heirlooms, and not for sale.

As throughout Southeast Asia, the Hoa (ethnic Chinese) merchants who dominated the commerce of Hoi An continued to identify themselves with their native province, and to this end built ★ **Chinese Assembly Halls** to act as community centres and places of worship. Five distinct Overseas Chinese communities lived in Hoi An – Guangdong, Fujian, Hainan, Chaozhou (Teochiu) and Hakka – and all except the latter had their own Assembly Hall (the Hakka were able to participate in the Chinese All Community Assembly). All five of these halls survive in Hoi An today, and all are worthy of a visit, though if time is limited the ★ **Fujian Assembly Hall** is probably the most interesting. Founded in the late 17th century, a new and elaborate triple-arched gateway was erected as recently as 1975.

Hoi An also has several small but interesting ★ **Temples** which are worth visiting. These include **Chua Ong**, also known as **Chua Quan Cong**, centrally located on Tran

Phu Street, which was established in 1653 and is dedicated to Quan Cong, a member of the Taoist pantheon who brings good luck and is the protective god of travellers. The **Tran Family Chapel** on Le Loi Street was established about two centuries ago as a shrine to the ancestors of the Tran family who moved from China to Vietnam around 1700. Once again, the building shows clear signs of Chinese influence, as does the **Truong Family Chapel** on a nearby side street running south of Phan Chu Trinh Street. The **Chuc Thanh Pagoda**, about 1km (½ mile) north of the town centre, is the oldest pagoda in Hoi An. Founded in 1454 by a Buddhist monk from China, the main sanctuary shelters a statue of the A Di Da Buddha (Amitabha, the Buddha of the Past), flanked by two Thich Ca Mau Ni Buddhas (Sakyamuni, the Buddha Gautama). **Phuoc Lam Pagoda**, founded in the mid-17th century, is dedicated to An Thiem, a denizen of Hoi An who became a monk aged eight before becoming a soldier and rising to the rank of general. In later life, feeling guilty for all those he had killed, he returned to Hoi An and swept the local market for 20 years to atone for his sins.

Other points of interest include the **Ma Nhat** or **Japanese Tombs** about 2km (1¼ miles) north of the town centre. The tombstone of the Japanese merchant Yajirobei, who died at Hoi An in 1647, faces northeast towards his homeland and is clearly inscribed with *kanji* characters; a few hundred metres away – it may be necessary to ask a local the exact whereabouts – is the tombstone of another Japanese, Masai by name, who died at Hoi An in 1629.

Finally, mention should be made of a surviving **French Quarter** dating back to the beginning of the 20th century, which may be found to the south of Phan Boi Chau Street, beside the river in the southeastern part of town.

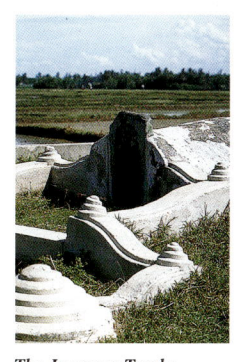

The Japanese Tombs

Visitor to the Tombs

Apsaras at Chien Dang Cham

Route 6

Champa and Central Coast

My Son – Tam Ky – Quang Ngai – My Lai – Qui Nhon – Thap Doi – Nha Trang – Po Nagar – Phan Rang – Po Klong Garai – Phan Tiet *See map on page 50*

Bathtime by the sea

The journey down Vietnam's long central coastline allows the traveller to laze on some of the country's finest beaches and enjoy a wide variety of fresh and delicious seafood. It is also a journey back in time. For over a thousand years the whole of this beautiful region belonged to the Chams, a seafaring people who built a great Hindu civilisation in the eastern lee of the Annamese Cordillera. Over the centuries, as the Vietnamese pressed inexorably south, Champa was gradually snuffed out, forcing many of its citizens to take refuge in nearby Cambodia. Had Champa survived, Indochina would now comprise four countries instead of three – but it was not to be. Today, little remains of this lost kingdom beyond the great brick towers that dot the countryside, and scattered communities of ethnic Chams, now a minority in a land they once ruled.

The Kingdom of Champa was established in or around the 2nd century AD. It's not certain where the Chams originated, though the fact that they were a seafaring people and that Cham is an Austronesian language strongly suggests links with the Malay-Polynesian world. For about a thousand years, from the 5th to the 15th centuries, the Chams flourished. At its apogee, Champa controlled the entire central coast of what would later become Vietnam, from the Hoanh Son Pass in the north (also known as the 'Gateway to Annam' on the frontier between Ha Tinh and

Quang Binh Provinces) to the region of Vung Tau in the south. The Chams soon became Hinduised through commercial contacts with India, and their country functioned as a rather loose confederation of five states named after regions of India – Indrapura (Quang Tri), Amaravati (Quang Nam), Vijaya (Binh Dinh), Kauthara (Nha Trang) and Panduranga (Phan Rang). The Chams were renowned sailors and notorious pirates who were almost constantly at war with their neighbours, the Viets to the north and the Khmers to the south and west. From the east – the ocean – they also faced periodic attack from China and from Java.

At the beginning of the 10th century Champa came under severe pressure from Dai Viet, which was beginning its long push to the south. In 1069 Indrapura was lost to the Viets, and by 1306 Champa's northern frontier had been pushed back to the Hai Van Pass with the loss of Amaravati. The process of Vietnamese expansion proved inexorable, with Vijaya falling in 1471 and Champa – now reduced to the rump kingdoms of Kauthara and Panduranga – effectively a broken power. Final absorption by Vietnam was delayed until the reign of Minh Mang in 1832, by which time the Vietnamese were already engaged in the conquest of the lower Cambodian regions of Prey Nokor (later renamed Saigon) and the Mekong Delta.

Thus Champa disappeared – but not so the Cham people. As their kingdom was swallowed piecemeal by Vietnam, so increasing numbers of Cham fled to neighbouring Cambodia, though others chose to remain under Vietnamese tutelage in their former homelands. Today there are as many as half a million 'Western Chams' in Cambodia, nearly all of whom adopted Islam centuries ago. In Vietnam the 'Eastern Chams' are fewer in number – perhaps 150,000 – and are divided between the Mekong Delta, where they are predominantly Muslim, and the central coast between Phan Rang and Phan Thiet (formerly Panduranga) where they are mainly Hindu. What is more, the artistic and religious legacy of Champa survives all along the central coast of Vietnam, from Da Nang (with its remarkable Cham Museum, *see page 51*) almost to Saigon, making an exploration of this region especially rewarding to the visitor.

Cham Museum sculpture

About 40km (25 miles) southwest of Hoi An, in the lee of the appropriately-named Hon Quap or Cat's Tooth Mountain, is ★★ **My Son**, site of the most significant Cham monuments in Vietnam. My Son was an important religious centre between the 4th and 13th centuries, serving as a spiritual counterpart to the nearby Amaravati capital **Simhapura** or **Tra Kieu**, little of which remains. Traces of around 70 temples and related structures may still be found at My Son, though only about 20 are

Nandi statue at My Son

One of the Cham Towers

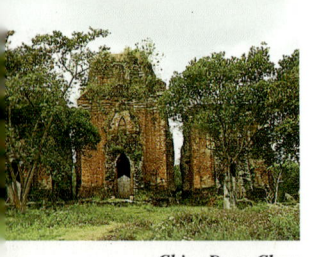

Chien Dang Cham

Cham Tower near Qui Nhon

still in good condition. The monuments are divided into 10 groups, the most important of which are Groups B, C and D – Group A having been almost completely destroyed by US bombing during the Second Indochina War. The most striking of the monuments are the famed ★★ **Cham Towers**, tall sanctuaries made of brick bonded together in a fashion which still puzzles the experts, for no bonding material is visible. The best explanation offered to date – though it is still uncertain – is that the Cham master-builders used a form of resin to 'glue' the bricks together.

The temples of Champa generally follow one basic design. They represent Mount Meru, the Hindu abode of the gods, and generally face east towards the rising sun. They are smaller than the temples of neighbouring Cambodia, chiefly because they are built with brick and limited use is made of stone lintels. The sanctum sanctorum – *kalan* in Cham – normally had a Shivalinga at its centre. Temples usually had three storeys and were plain inside. The outer walls, brick and sandstone, were carved with magnificent skill after construction had been completed. At the height of Champa's power and glory, the roofs of at least some of the temples at My Son were covered with a fine layer of pure gold, which must have fairly blazed under the hot tropical sun.

The coast of central Vietnam is dotted with Cham Towers from Da Nang south to Phan Thiet. Near **Tam Ky**, the capital of Quang Nam Province, just 62km (39 miles) south of Da Nang, three towers dating from the 11th century rise from a walled enclosure at **Chien Dang Cham**. Here there are fine sculptures of creatures from Hindu mythology – *naga*, *kinnaree*, *garuda*, *hamsa* and *makara* – as well as more mundane images of dancers, musicians and elephants. Also near Tam Ky is the important Cham site of **Khuong My**, a temple complex dating from the 10th century which is renowned for the richness of its decorated pillars, pilasters and arches.

Highway 1 south of Tam Ky passes through the quiet provincial town of **Quang Ngai**. There's not much to see here, and there are no major Cham monuments – but 14km (9 miles) northeast of town is the village of **My Lai**, site of the infamous massacre of Vietnamese peasants by US forces on 16 March 1968. The village was supposedly a Viet Cong stronghold, yet the residents turned out to be unarmed civilians. Several hundred people, including women and children, were shot to death that day. The American public didn't find out about My Lai until the autumn of 1969, when a former soldier decided to write to government officials and force the truth out into the light.

The coastal city of **Qui Nhon**, 156km (98 miles) further south, is more of a fishing port than a beach resort.

It's a convenient place to overnight, however, and there are further souvenirs of Champa in the vicinity. Just 2km (1¼ miles) north of town stand the two Cham Towers of **Thap Doi**, which may be visited en route to the ruins of **Cha Ban** some 26km (16 miles) away. Cha Ban was the capital of Vijaya from about 1000 to 1471. In the latter year the greatest military disaster ever to befall Champa occurred as the forces of Viet King Le Thanh Ton fought their way into the fortified city. Vietnamese sources claim 60,000 Cham defenders were killed, and 30,000 – including the Cham King and 50 members of his family – taken captive. Today the delicately ornamented sandstone pilasters of ★ **Canh Tien**, the 'Bronze Tower', rise from the centre of the fortified enclosure, but little else survives.

Follow Highway 1 southwards for a further 240km (150 miles) to ★★ **Nha Trang** – there are no significant Cham monuments en route, but there are fine views of the South China Sea and especially of ★ **Van Phong Bay**. Nha Trang is an attractive, medium-sized city of about 200,000 people with one of the best beaches in Vietnam. The waters are clear and clean, and the offshore islands are ideal for snorkelling, scuba diving and fishing. Nha Trang has a pleasant, laid-back feel to it. Just 2km (1¼ miles) out of town the well-preserved and restored ★★ **Po Nagar Cham Towers** rise on a low hill. This is one of the most important Cham sites in Vietnam, and dates back to the 8th century. The temple is dedicated to the goddess Yang Ino Po Nagar and was originally constructed by the Kramuka Vamsh or 'Betel Nut Clan' rulers of Kauthara. Of the original eight towers, four remain standing; there is also a *mandapa* or meditation hall, and a modern museum.

Highway 1 continues south curving around Cam Ranh Bay – one of the finest natural harbours in Southeast Asia and, in Cold War times, a scene of rivalry between the US and Soviet navies – to reach, after 105km (66 miles), the twin towns of **Phan Rang** and **Thap Cham**.

Known chiefly for the excellence of the local grapes and as a railway repair yard, there isn't a lot to do or see here, but 7km (4 miles) out of town, along Highway 20 to Dalat, stands ★★ **Po Klong Garai**. By now the visitor may well have seen enough Cham Towers, but it's well worth visiting these well-restored 13th-century monuments, not least because this region was once part of Panduranga, the last Cham Kingdom, and many Chams still live in the area. As a consequence, Po Klong Garai is very much a 'living' temple complex, used by local Chams as a place of worship and to hold festivals, as is **Po Rome** just south of town. A sizeable community of Chams also survives 146km (91 miles) further south, around the small fishing port of **Pan Thiet**.

Nha Trang beach

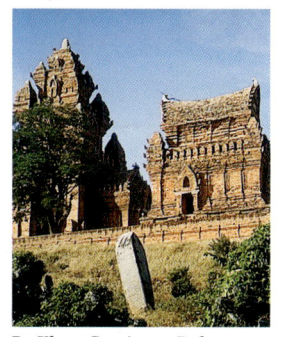

Po Klong Garai near Dalat

Downtown Dalat

Route 7

Dalat

See map on page 50

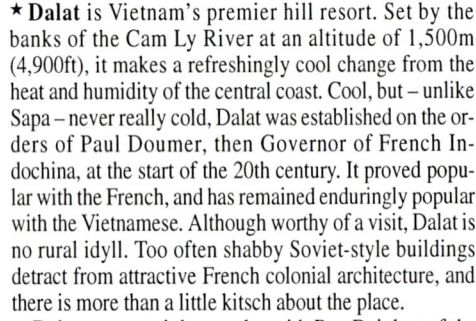

★ **Dalat** is Vietnam's premier hill resort. Set by the banks of the Cam Ly River at an altitude of 1,500m (4,900ft), it makes a refreshingly cool change from the heat and humidity of the central coast. Cool, but – unlike Sapa – never really cold, Dalat was established on the orders of Paul Doumer, then Governor of French Indochina, at the start of the 20th century. It proved popular with the French, and has remained enduringly popular with the Vietnamese. Although worthy of a visit, Dalat is no rural idyll. Too often shabby Soviet-style buildings detract from attractive French colonial architecture, and there is more than a little kitsch about the place.

Dalat was certainly popular with Bao Dai, last of the Nguyen Emperors (1926–45), who enjoyed hunting in the surrounding hills and indulging his taste for high living amongst the French and Vietnamese élite. To celebrate his affection for the hill station, the former emperor ordered the construction of a large villa set amidst pine trees about 2km (1¼ miles) out of town. Completed in 1933, the villa – generally known as **Bao Dai's Summer Palace** – is open to the public, and visitors can even stay here for US$40 a night. That said, there isn't a great deal of interest in the villa. The former imperial living quarters are on the first floor, and here one can see busts of Bao Dai and his father Khai Dinh, together with assorted family pictures.

Bao Dai's Summer Palace

Dalat has a number of pagodas and temples, including the **Thien Vuong Pagoda** about 5km (3 miles) southeast of town on Khe Sanh Road. Set on a pine-covered hill, the yellow-coloured pagoda was built by the local Chaozhou (Teochiu) community in 1958 and is chiefly remarkable for housing three 4-m (13-ft) high standing Buddha images made of gilded sandalwood. These images – given by a British Buddhist and sent from Hong Kong – are said to be the largest sandalwood Buddhas in Vietnam. About 1km (½ mile) southwest of the town centre, **Lam Ty Ni Pagoda** was established in 1961 and is set amidst pleasant flower gardens. The attraction here, however, is less the temple than the person of Vien Thuc, the resident monk, who is also a poet and artist of local renown. Mr Thuc welcomes visitors and will readily show them around the temple and the gardens that he tends with great care. Hundreds of his poems and paintings are on display in and around the temple, and they're all for sale! About 1km (½ mile) to the north of town, **Linh Son Pagoda** was established in 1938 and is known for its huge bell, said to be made of bronze mixed with gold.

Family fun at the flower gardens

It's pleasant to take a stroll around central Dalat, especially in the early evening. The town isn't large, and it retains a distinctly Gallic flavour, especially in the streets of the ★ **French Quarter** between the cinema and Phan Dinh Phung Street. Also reminiscent of the colonial period is the pastel pink **Dalat Cathedral** on Tran Phu Road. Completed in 1942, it is dedicated to St Nicolas and boasts a 47-m (153-ft) high spire and stained glass windows.

Dalat Cathedral

There are several noted beauty spots around Dalat. **Ho Than Tho** or the 'Lake of Sighs', 6km (4 miles) northeast of town, is a popular picnic spot surrounded by forested hills. There are several small restaurants near the lake, and you can hire horses to ride in the area. About 13km (8 miles) out of town along Highway 20 to Phan Rang, the ★ **Prenn Falls** are a popular local attraction. The water falls 15m (50ft) from a wide ridge into a deep pool below. It's possible to walk under the lip of the falls, permitting a fine view of the pool and the surrounding forest. During the monsoon rains the falls roar and turn a frothy, milky-brown colour.

About 12km (7 miles) northwest of Dalat, situated at the base of **Lang Bian Mountain**, is a group of nine small settlements which make up **Lat Village**. This is an excellent place to go if you wish to see local hill peoples, still commonly referred to by the French term **Montagnards**. Five of the settlements are inhabited by people of the Lat minority whilst the other four are inhabited by members of related minority groups, the Ma and the Chill. The villagers, who make a living by growing dry rice, coffee, beans and yams, are known for their pottery and ironworking skills. A permit is needed to visit the villages. To obtain one visit the Immigration Police in Dalat.

Prenn Falls

Express delivery, Ho Chi Minh City

River view

Veteran of the times

Route 8

Ho Chi Minh City (Saigon)

See map on page 62–3

Saigon is a sprawling urban mass, larger than Hanoi, the nation's capital, but somehow less cohesive and certainly with a far shorter history. Until the 17th century it was no more than a small Khmer fishing settlement called Prey Nokor – a name still widely applied by Cambodian nationalists to the city today. Then, when a group of Chinese refugees from the Qing Empire arrived in the region, the Cambodian governor turned for advice and help to the Nguyen lords of Hue. The price of settling the Chinese and restoring order was Vietnamese suzerainty. Later, the city expanded to join with the nearby Chinese settlement of Cholon – Saigon has always had a strong Chinese flavour to it. In 1859 the city was seized by France and soon became the chief city of the French colony of Cochinchina. Briefly, between 1956 and 1975, Saigon functioned as the capital of the anti-communist Republic of Vietnam. After the communist seizure of power in 1975, however, it was once again overshadowed by its older and more distinguished rival, Hanoi – a development symbolised by the change of name to Ho Chi Minh City in 1976.

The Communist authorities also extended the municipal boundaries so that 'Ho Chi Minh City' is now a small province extending from the South China Sea almost as far as the Cambodian frontier. As a consequence – and perhaps also as an expression of regional identity – most southerners continue to refer to downtown Ho Chi Minh City as 'Saigon', whilst the traditional Chinatown area further to the west remains generally known as 'Cholon'.

Saigon

Ho Chi Minh City is newer, larger and brasher than Hanoi. Downtown Saigon is as much a creation of France as of Vietnam, but the city's rather distinguished colonial style acquired something of a glitzy veneer between 1954 and 1975, when Saigon served as the capital of the US-backed Republic of Vietnam. The Saigonese are a lively people, seemingly intent on 'getting ahead', with little time to spend worrying about the past.

A good place to start an exploration of the downtown area is the **Waterfront**. Here one can watch the hustle and bustle of life on the Saigon River, as small craft jostle for space with larger ocean-going ships and hydrofoils bound for Vung Tau. Running northwest from the river, busy Dong Khoi – known as Rue Catinat under the French and Tu Do during the American years – is the heart of the old **French Quarter** and leads to **Notre Dame Cathedral ❶**, a towering redbrick structure erected by the French in 1883. Other colonial buildings worth visiting in the vicinity are the splendid **General Post Office**, just to the east of the cathedral, the **Municipal Theatre** on Lam Son Square sandwiched between two of Saigon's most distinguished hotels, the **Continental** and the **Caravelle**; and especially the magnificent gingerbread **Hôtel de Ville** at the northern end of Nguyen Hue Boulevard. This is Graham Greene land *par excellence*, and the haunt of a thousand reporters and photographers during the interminable war years.

Downtown Saigon isn't known for its temples, but northwest of the colonial heart of the city, along Dien Bien Phu boulevard, there are two worth visiting. **Chua Ngoc Huang ❷** or 'Pagoda of the Jade Emperor' is at the northern end of Dien Bien Phu near Rach Thi Creek. Built in 1909, this is a spectacularly colourful Chinese temple dedicated to Ngoc Huang, Jade Emperor of the Taoist pantheon. At the junction of Dien Bien Phu and Huyen Than Quan is **Xa Loi Pagoda ❸**, a Vietnamese temple lined with paintings of scenes from the life of the Buddha.

Most of Saigon's museums are located in the central downtown area, and some at least merit a visit – though, a quarter of a century after the event, it might be thought that excessive emphasis is placed on the Indochina Wars. Thus the **War Remnants Museum** (formerly called The Museum of Chinese and American War Crimes), housed in the old USIS building at 28 Vo Van Tan, manages to combine the tired clichés of communist doublespeak with truly disturbing exhibits, such as photographs of the My Lai massacre, the effects of chemical defoliants, torture and general brutality. It takes a strong stomach to look at many of the photographs on display, but the overall effect – whilst emphasising the brutality of war – is both shallow

Hôtel de Ville

War Remnants Museum

Reunification Palace

and one-sided. Also rooted firmly in the recent past, the **Revolutionary Museum** at 65 Ly Tu Trong provides more evidence of French, US and Chinese duplicity and barbarism. Information is generally given in Vietnamese only, but the gist is clear enough. The **Military Museum** ❹, on the corner of Le Duan and Nguyen Binh Khiem, houses a collection of military weaponry from the USA, China and the former Soviet Union; one prized exhibit is the tank which smashed through the gate of the Presidential Palace (now the Reunification Palace) on 30 April, 1975, symbolising the fall of the south. In similar vein though less well supplied with hardware is the No 7 Army Museum near **Tan Son Nhat** Airport. There are also two museums dedicated to revolutionary leaders, the inevitable **Ho Chi Minh Museum** on Nguyen That Than, and the **Ton Duc Thang Museum** – named for Ho's successor as president, Ton Duc Thang, who died in 1980 – on Ton Duc Thang.

Away from revolutionary struggle, the ★ **History Museum** ❺ on Nguyen Binh Kiem initially misleads as the visitor is confronted by a large statue of Ho Chi Minh in the entrance hall. Within, however, there's a more orthodox display, featuring artefacts illustrating the evolution

Painting incense sticks

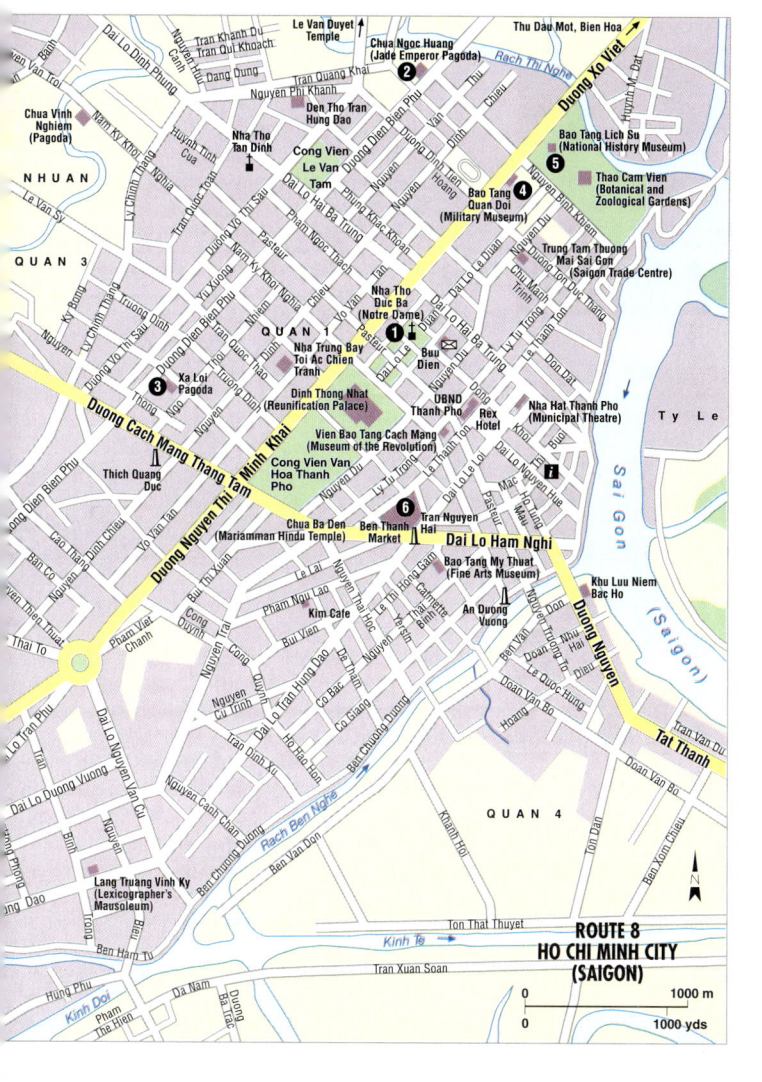

**ROUTE 8
HO CHI MINH CITY
(SAIGON)**

Choices at Ben Thanh Market

Cholon

of Vietnamese culture from Dong Son civilisation, through Oc Eo and Champa to pre-colonial Vietnam. Also worthy of a visit is the ★ **Art Museum** on Pho Duc Chinh. Housed in an attractive yellow and white colonial building, the exhibits here include contemporary Vietnamese art on the 1st floor, abstract art on the 2nd floor, and revolutionary art – featuring Vietnamese interpretations of Socialist Realism – also on the 2nd floor. Upstairs on the 3rd floor are displays of artefacts from Oc Eo, Cambodia and Champa. The Cham collection is particularly impressive, being surpassed only by the displays of the Cham Museum in Da Nang and the Musée Guimet in Paris.

Right in the heart of downtown Saigon, ★ **Ben Thanh Market** ❻ seems to symbolise the freewheeling, commercially driven spirit of Ho Chi Minh City. The largest covered market in town, it is packed with stalls selling all manner of wares and thousands of busy, haggling shoppers. Most locals will be shopping for fresh food or clothing, but there are also souvenirs for sale – conical *non la* hats, silk *ao dai* costumes, silk-screened T-shirts, coffee from Dalat and a range of imitation antiquities.

Cholon

About 6km (4 miles) west of central Saigon lies the densely inhabited settlement of ★ **Cholon**, Ho Chi Minh City's Chinatown. From the end of the 18th century, ethnic Chinese 'Hoa' hailing mostly from the coastal provinces of southern China settled in this region, establishing a township physically and ethnically distinct from nearby Saigon. Gradually, as the two settlements expanded, they began to merge – when Norman Lewis passed through Saigon in 1950 he found Cholon 'swollen so enormously as to become its grotesque Siamese twin'. Today the merger is complete and Cholon – the name in Vietnamese means, appropriately enough, 'Big Market' – forms an alternative, if less stylish, town centre for Ho Chi Minh City.

Cholon is best approached from Saigon by Tran Hung Dao, which runs directly from Ben Thanh Market to central Cholon. The attractions of Cholon are easy to enumerate – people and temples just about sum it up. It's a great place for people watching, whether by the grimy godowns and boathouses of the waterfront, or at busy **Binh Tay Market**. The Chinese presence is readily apparent, both in the characters of many shop signs, and in the faces and dress style of the people. Once a *very* Chinese place, Hoa influence and numbers declined markedly during the first two decades of communist rule, initially because of unpopular socialist economic policies, and subsequently because of anti-Chinese sentiment. In recent years, however, many Hoa have returned, and once again Saigon's 'Big Market' is evocative of the Middle Kingdom.

Inside the Thien Hau Pagoda

Set in the heart of Cholon, ★ **Nghia An Hoi Quan Pagoda** ❼ serves the local Chaozhou (Teochiu) community and is chiefly notable for its gilded woodwork. Its shady interior is dominated by huge hanging spirals of incense said to burn for one month. There are usually a number of pious worshippers at prayer, and people call at all times of the day to shake the fortune sticks and read their future. Just across the road, the 19th-century ★ **Tam Son Hoi Quan Pagoda** ❽ serves the local Fujian community and is dedicated to Me Sanh, the Goddess of Fertility. Many local Hoa and Viet women come to this faded but richly ornamented temple to pray for children. A few steps to the northwest will bring the visitor to ★ **Thien Hau Pagoda** ❾, built in the early 19th century to serve Cholon's substantial Guangdong community, which has recently been renovated. This temple is dedicated to Thien Hau, a goddess venerated as the patron saint of seafarers, and Hoa migrants arriving at Cholon by sea would have made this their first port of call to give thanks for safe passage. Also in this central area is the easily distinguished **Cholon Mosque**, built by migrants from the tiny former French colonies of Pondicherry and Mahé in India.

North of Cholon by the southern shore of Dam Sen Lake, ★ **Giac Vien Pagoda** is one of the oldest temples in Ho Chi Minh City. Founded around 1800, Nguyen Emperor Gia Long is said to have worshipped here. Although quite difficult to reach – a taxi is advisable – this serene temple is one of the most interesting in town. Still further north, in the rather dreary suburb of Tan Binh, ★ **Giac Lam Pagoda** (1744) is said to be the oldest temple in the Saigon-Cholon region. Although primarily a Mahayana Buddhist temple, Taoist and Confucian deities are also represented. It was last renovated in 1900, so – by the upstart standards of Saigon – this is a venerable place indeed!

Tam Son Hoi Quan Pagoda

Excursions from Ho Chi Minh City

Vung Tau – Tunnels of Cu Chi – Tay Ninh – Nui Ba Den
See map below

There are two worthwhile trips in the vicinity of Ho Chi Minh City. To the southeast the seaside resort town of Vung Tau offers sun, sand, swimming and seafood. To the northwest are the amazing Tunnels of Cu Chi as well as, a short distance beyond, Tay Ninh, site of the Great Temple of the extraordinary Cao Dai religion. It's possible to use local transport on both these tours, but it makes more sense to charter a taxi, especially if you intend combining Cu Chi and Tay Ninh in a single day trip.

Boats and beach at Vung Tau

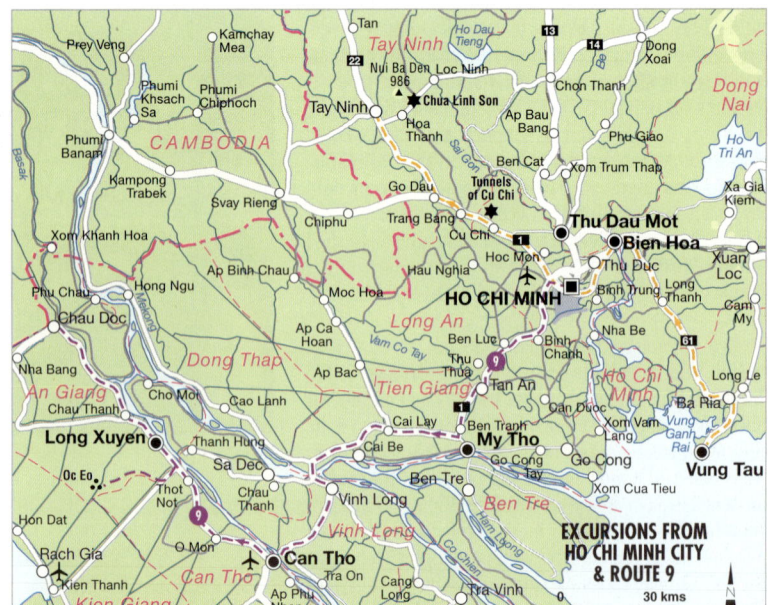

The resort town of **Vung Tau** – in colonial times it was known as Cap St Jacques – lies at the tip of a triangular peninsula jutting into the sea near the mouth of the Saigon River. It can be reached by minibus or taxi in around 2 hours; alternatively – and more enjoyably – hydrofoils leave from the junction of the Saigon River and the Kinh Ben Creek in central Saigon on a regular basis. The 90-minute journey provides glimpses of everyday life in the small riverine fishing villages en route. Vung Tau or 'Boat Bay' has a contradictory feel to it. A resort town which is also partly industrialised, it is home to a major Viet-

Russian offshore oil company and a large fishing fleet. The beaches are unexceptional by Vietnamese standards. The main appeal of the place must be its proximity to Ho Chi Minh City and excellent fresh seafood.

Located 35km (22 miles) northwest of Saigon, the district of **Cu Chi** is famous for its remarkable underground ★ **tunnel network**. During the Second Indochina War, the National Liberation Front – better known as the Viet Cong – established a vast network of underground passages, dormitories, kitchens, munitions factories and hospitals stretching from the fringes of Saigon to the frontier with Cambodia, with a total length of more than 250km (156 miles). In places this complex was three storeys deep, so even the much-feared B52 'Arclight' strikes were generally unable to destroy the third, lowest level tunnels.

Today two sections of the Cu Chi tunnel network have been renovated and opened to visitors, one at Ben Dinh and the other at nearby Ben Duoc. They are easily visited on a side trip from Highway 22 to Tay Ninh – the easiest thing is to charter a taxi to Tay Ninh and arrange with the driver to stop at Cu Chi either on the way out or on the way back. Usually your guide will start by taking you to an area of brush or low trees and asking you to try and locate an entrance to the tunnels. It's not easy – and most Westerners couldn't fit through the entrance even if they found it. Not to worry though, as the industrious Vietnamese, proud of their military achievement in surviving at Cu Chi and anxious to bring in tourist dollars, have enlarged several sections of tunnel to suit larger Western frames. The tunnels are still narrow, humid and bat-filled, however, so few visitors will want to stay long underground. The very idea of hiding in such tunnels during a heavy bombing raid doesn't bear thinking about.

★★ **Tay Ninh**, about 50km (31 miles) beyond Cu Chi and 96km (60 miles) from central Saigon, is the headquarters of Vietnam's – perhaps, indeed, the world's – strangest religion. Founded in 1926 by a Vietnamese civil servant and mystic named Ngo Minh Chieu, **Cao Dai** or 'High Tower' (a Taoist epithet for the Supreme God) is a syncretic philosophy which incorporates a strong strand of Vietnamese nationalism. Cao Dai draws upon traditional Vietnamese religions for its moral precepts (Confucianism), its occult practices (Taoism) and its belief in the doctrines of karma and rebirth (Buddhism). The hierarchical organisation of the church – which includes a pope as supreme patriarch, archbishops and cardinals – is adopted from Roman Catholicism, as indeed is the Cao Dai proclivity for saints. The latter embrace a broad church of religious, cultural and political

Tunnel opening

Cao Dai Great Temple, Tay Ninh

Cao Dai veterans

God, the all-seeing eye

Dragon-swathed pillars

figures including the Buddha, Confucius, Jesus Christ, Pericles, Julius Caesar, Joan of Arc, Napoleon Bonaparte, William Shakespeare, Victor Hugo and Sun Yat-sen. Even the Prophet Muhammad finds a place. God is represented as an all-seeing eye in a triangle, giving Cao Dai temples something of a cabalistic feel. Worship involves elaborate rituals and festivals.

Within a year of its founding Cao Dai, had more than 25,000 adherents, and by the 1950s between 12 and 15 percent of all South Vietnamese were followers. By the end of the First Indochina War in 1954, Tay Ninh Province had become an almost independent Cao Dai fiefdom. The Cao Dai remained generally aloof from the struggle in the Second Indochina War, and as a consequence suffered severe persecution following the communist seizure of power in 1975. Today, matters are much more relaxed, and it is estimated that there are 3 million followers of Cao Dai in Vietnam, worshipping at more than 400 temples throughout the southern and central provinces.

The extraordinary ★★ **Than That Cao Dai** or **Cao Dai Great Temple**, also known as the 'Holy See', stands 4km (2½ miles) east of Tay Ninh in the village of Long Hoa. Prayers are conducted four times daily at 6am, noon, 6pm and midnight, but visitors should try to attend the noon session, as the Cao Dai authorities prefer this, and also permit – even encourage – photography. The temple, which rises in nine levels, is elaborately – some would say gaudily – decorated. Certainly it is surreal, a pastiche of divine eyes, Cao Dai saints, dragon-swathed pillars and vaulted ceilings. Various celebrated writers have penned their impressions of this unique structure, which strives to combine Catholic cathedral with Buddhist temple. To Graham Greene it was a 'Walt Disney fantasia of the East', whilst Norman Lewis saw it as 'fun-fair architecture in extreme form… one expected continually to hear bellowing laughter relayed from some nearby Tunnel of Love'.

Note that men should enter the Great Temple through an entrance to the right of the main portal, whilst women should enter from the left. You will be greeted and shown around by members of the Cao Dai clergy, male and female, who are dressed in elaborate costumes.

Nui Ba Den or 'Black Lady Mountain' is an 986-m (3204-ft) high hill rising out of the rice paddies about 15km (9 miles) northeast of Tay Ninh. Because of its symmetrical shape, and because it stands alone, it dominates the countryside and has become a symbol of Tay Ninh Province. It is possible to climb Nui Ba Den, visiting a Buddhist temple en route. There are fine views of the fertile, rice-growing plains from the summit; and on a clear day it is possible to see far into neighbouring Cambodia.

Casting nets on the Mekong

Route 9

The Mekong Delta

Mekong River – My Tho – Vinh Long – Can Tho – Long Xuyen – Oc Eo – Chau Doc – Chau Giang
See map on page 66

Broad, lush and absolutely flat, the great delta of the ★★**Mekong River** forms the southernmost part of the country, extending to **Mui Ca Mau** – Vietnam's Cap Finistère, where the waters of the South China Sea meet those of the Gulf of Thailand. The vast delta region is made up of rich alluvial silt carried down by the floodwaters of the Mekong from Cambodia, Laos and Thailand. So regular is this process that the delta is growing at a rate of about 75m (245ft) per year, extending both the shoreline and the rich farmlands known as 'Vietnam's Rice Bowl'. A visit to this region enables the traveller to explore shaded waterways and floating markets by boat, see relics of the ancient Funanese city of Oc Eo, and visit the delta's Khmer Buddhist temples and Cham Muslim mosques.

A convenient first stop in the delta is **My Tho**, a sprawling market town by the banks of the Ham Luong branch of the Mekong, just 60km (38 miles) southwest of Ho Chi Minh City. After bustling Saigon, My Tho is pleasantly quiet and a good place to overnight while taking a boat trip to explore local waterways and islands. In My Tho itself, the huge **market** provides an insight into local lifestyles. The elaborate ★**Cao Dai Temple** is worth visiting, as are the pastel-coloured colonial period **Catholic Church** and the immaculate **Vinh Trang Buddhist Pagoda**.

Pushing deeper into the Mekong Delta, the next stop is **Vinh Long**, about 60km (38 miles) southwest of My Tho in a journey which necessitates a ferry crossing of the

River life at Vinh Long

broad Tien Giang, or Upper Mekong River. This is another possible overnight stop as there are several adequate hotels and good restaurants. Vinh Long is famous for its picturesque ★ **Cai Be Floating Market** about an hour by boat from the town centre. The market functions from around 5am to 5pm, but it's best to visit in the early morning. Another worthwhile boat trip is to nearby ★ **Anh Binh Island**. Easily reached by small boats available for the purpose, the island is very fertile and supports many vegetable gardens and orchards. It's pleasant to sail or stroll around, watching the bobbing *non la* conical hats of the local women as they tend their plots. About 2km (1 mile) south of town, by the banks of the Rach Long Canal, stands **Van Thanh Mieu**, a large temple dedicated to Confucius.

Raking rice at Can Tho

Can Tho, 34km (21 miles) and one major ferry crossing southwest of Vinh Long, is the largest town and de facto 'capital' of the Mekong Delta. There's a domestic airport set amidst the myriad waterways, and boat or ferry connections can be made to almost anywhere in the delta. Here, too, the presence of Vietnam's substantial Khmer minority begins to make itself felt. **Munirangsyaram Pagoda** on Hoa Binh Street is the centre of Theravada Buddhism in the city, which has a Cambodian population of around 2,500. There are two interesting floating markets within easy striking distance of Can Tho – ★ **Cai Rang**, about 5km (3 miles) southeast of the city, and ★ **Phong Dien**, possibly the most traditional and least motorised floating market in the delta, situated about 20km (12 miles) to the southwest. Can Tho is another good place to stay overnight, as the accommodation available is the best in the delta and there are numerous good restaurants.

At the fish market in Chau Doc

About 60km (38 miles) northwest of Can Tho along a minor road, the town of **Long Xuyen** has little to offer, but is a necessary transit point on the way northwest to the Cambodian frontier. Nearby are the ruins of **Oc Eo**, an important trading port of the Kingdom of Funan, which dominated much of the Gulf of Siam coast and the Mekong Delta in the 2nd–6th centuries AD. Little remains of this once great settlement – the passage of time and shifting mudflats of the Mekong have obliterated all but pottery shards and some pilings. What survives of Funan culture is better viewed at the **History Museum** and **Art Museum** in **Ho Chi Minh City** and the **History Museum** in **Hanoi**.

Beyond Long Xuyen, the road continues northwest along the banks of the Hau Giang or Bassac River – also known as the 'Lower Mekong' – passing through vast reaches of rice paddy towards the border with Cambodia's Takeo Province.

Close by the frontier, on the south side of the Hau Giang, lies the city of **Chau Doc**. Until the mid-18th century

Chau Doc, like much of the Mekong Delta, was under Cambodian suzerainty – to this day Cambodians refer to the Mekong Delta region of Vietnam as *Kampuchea Krom* or 'Lower Cambodia'. Chau Doc still retains a border atmosphere, with an interesting racial mix. The town is predominantly Viet, but sustains sizeable Hoa (Chinese), Cham and especially Khmer minorities. The religious mix is still more eclectic – there are Vietnamese and Chinese Mahayana Buddhists, Cambodian Theravada Buddhists, Chinese and Vietnamese Catholics, Cham Muslims, Vietnamese and Khmer Cao Dai and – strangest of all – Hoa Hao, followers of the second major religious sect indigenous to the Mekong Delta.

The Hoa Hao derive their designation from the small village of the same name some 20km (12 miles) east of Chau Doc. An austere and rather ascetic doctrine, Hoa Hao advocates a return to the Theravada ideal of personal salvation combined with aspects of Confucianism and Ancestor Worship. The Hoa Hao movement was born in the 1930s and – like the Cao Dai – soon developed a mundane political agenda which was both anti-French and anti-communist. Suppressed in turn by the French, the Viet Cong and (after 1975) by the communist government, Hoa Hao still claims around 1½ million followers, mainly around Chau Doc. Hoa Hao men often wear long beards and tie their hair up in a tight bun. Adherents of the sect have their own flag, maroon in colour, and their own special holidays.

The main Cham Muslim area of Chau Doc is across the river in **Chau Giang District**. Stilted wooden houses line the riverbank, while the men sport white prayer caps and sarongs. The Chau Giang skyline is dominated by the twin domes and minaret of **Masjid Mubarak**, one of several mosques in the area. Visitors are welcome, but should be properly dressed and avoid entering during prayers.

Relaxation for a monk

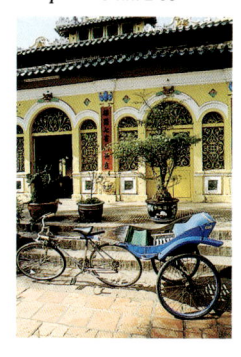

Temple in Chau Doc

Cham Muslim

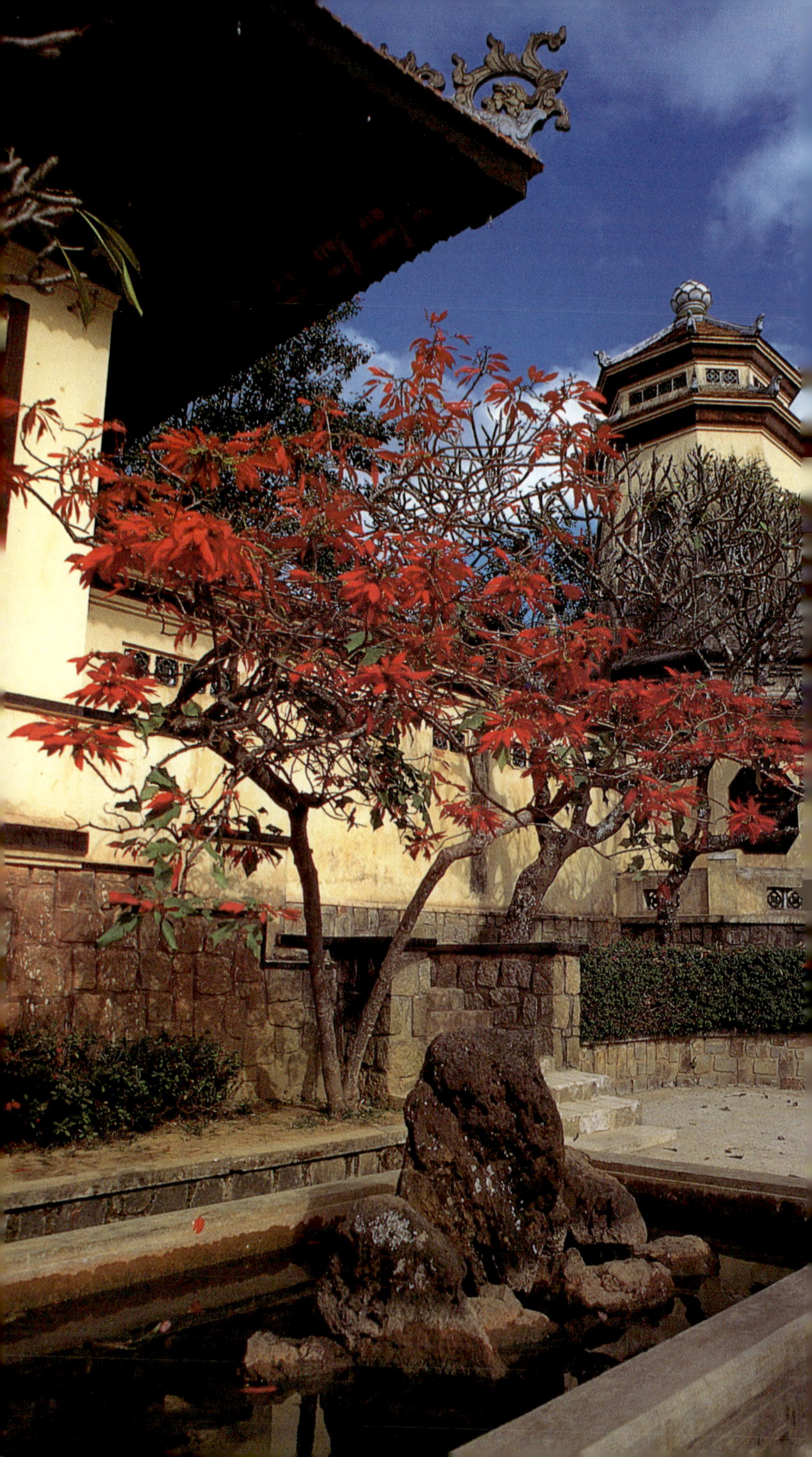

Vietnamese Temple Architecture

Vietnamese Buddhist Temples are similar to, and yet distinct from, their Chinese equivalents. The Vietnamese pagoda is usually single-storeyed rather than multi-tiered. Most have a sacred pond, usually replete with sacred turtles, a bell tower, and a garden. In front of the pagoda there is often a white statue of Avalokitesvara, in her feminine Chinese incarnation as The Goddess of Mercy, known in Vietnamese as *Quan The Am Bo Tat*, or 'Kuan Yin Bodhisattva'. She is often depicted holding her adopted son and standing on a lotus leaf – a symbol of purity.

The main building of the pagoda consists of several rooms. At the front are three doors, opened only for major religious festivals. Behind them lie a front hall, a central hall, and the main altar hall, usually arranged in ascending levels. Behind the temple, or to the side, are living quarters for monks or nuns. There will also usually be one or more subsidiary altar rooms specifically dedicated to the rites of ancestor worship.

Mahayana temples are distinguishable from their Theravada equivalents by the lavish use of dragon *(long)* rather than snake *(naga)* imagery. These are not the dangerous, destructive creatures of Western mythology, but the noble and beneficial dragons of imperial Chinese tradition. Look for them outside on the eaves and the apex of main roofs; inside they may be twined around supporting pillars, holding up altars and guarding doorways.

Inside the main sanctuary are representations of three Buddhas. These are *A Di Da*, or Amitabha, the Buddha of the past; *Thich Ca Mau Ni*, or Sakyamuni, the historic Buddha, Siddhartha Gautama; and *Di Lac*, or Maitreya, the Buddha of the future. Buddhas are distinguished by their long earlobes, an *urna*, or third eye, in their forehead, and their tightly curled hair. They are usually represented in one of the classical *mudras*, or attitudes, and seated on a throne, often in lotus form. Close by will be statues of the eight *Kim Cang*, or Genies of the Cardinal Directions, as well as various *La Han*, or Arhats, and *Bo Tat*, or Bodhisattvas. These are usually depicted as princes, wearing rich robes and crowns or head-dresses.

General decorative images to look for, besides dragons, include swastika motifs and the yin-yang symbol of Taoism symbolising the duality, or female and male elements, of existence. Chinese characters, too, although long abandoned by modern written Vietnamese, remain *de rigueur* in the spirit world. Sometimes, in temples where Taoist influences are strong, a separate altar may be set aside for Taoist divinities such as *Ngoc Hoang*, the Jade Emperor, and *Thien Hau Thanh Mau*, the Queen of Heaven.

Opposite: Linh Son Pagoda in Dalat

The Marble Mountain Pagoda is multi-tiered

The Enlightened One

Music and Theatre

Music

Traditional music in Saigon

Traditional Vietnamese music combines indigenous techniques thought to date back to the Dong Son period with Chinese influences and, through the Hinduised Kingdom of Champa, Indian musical forms. The resultant mix, which is technically very complex, is based on a five-tone scale in contrast to the eight-tone scale generally used in the West. Traditional Vietnamese instruments include wind instruments, string instruments, zithers and drums; they are often accompanied by song. An excellent place to see and hear traditional Vietnamese music is at the Temple of Literature in Hanoi.

Contemporary music in Vietnam has inevitably been influenced by Chinese, Thai and Western pop music. The resultant Viet Pop is known as 'Yellow Music'.

Theatre

Traditional Vietnamese theatre, known as *Hat Cheo* or 'Popular Opera', has its origins in the rice-farming culture of the Red River Delta. Performances, which are usually staged in front of a village community house or Buddhist pagoda, generally recount popular legends or concentrate on everyday affairs of the rulers and the ruled. *Hat Cheo* is traditionally rather anti-establishment and can be very satirical.

Hat Tuong was introduced from China in the 13th century and draws heavily on classical Chinese opera. Originally a theatre of the élite, it is essentially still a theatre of the moral and social status quo.

Hat Cai Luong or 'Renewed Theatre' developed in southern Vietnam at the beginning of the 20th century. It uses the vernacular language and employs techniques adapted from the European theatrical tradition.

Water Puppetry

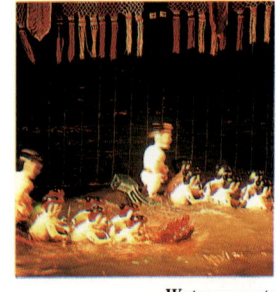

Water puppets

Roi Nuoc or Water Puppetry, a form of entertainment unique to Vietnam, originated in the Red River Delta of northern Vietnam more than a thousand years ago. The puppets are carved from the hard, water-resistant wood of the fig tree to represent both traditional rural lifestyles (farmers, buffaloes, ducks, officials) and mythical creatures (dragons, phoenixes, unicorns).

Standing concealed behind the watery stage, themselves waist-deep in water, the puppeteers use a complicated system of pulleys and poles to manoeuvre their wooden charges – which can weigh up to 20kg (45lb) each. Meanwhile a traditional orchestra playing flutes, drums, xylophones, gongs and various stringed instruments provides appropriate music to accompany the mythical storytelling.

Festivals

Most festivals in Vietnam can be traced to the country's close links with Chinese cultural traditions and follow the lunar calendar. In addition to the major nationwide celebrations, there are many smaller local festivals, especially in the Red River Delta where the Viet nation has its origins. Perhaps the best known and loved of all Vietnamese festivals is Tet, the Lunar New Year, a celebration marked for centuries by the explosion of a million firecrackers. Though these have been banned to prevent injury, Tet is still a pretty noisy occasion as the Vietnamese celebrate with drums and tape recordings of firecrackers! For details of secular public holidays, *see page 89*

January: January 1: *Tet Duong Lich* or New Year's Day.
January/February: The first to seventh days of the first lunar month: *Tet Nguyen Dan*, or *Tet*, the Vietnamese (and Chinese) Lunar New Year. After a tumultuous initial celebration, Tet becomes more of a family affair. On the fifth day of the first lunar month, Tay Son marks the Tay Son Peasant Rising against the Trinh and Nguyen Lords. Celebrated in Tay Son district in the Central Highlands. On the fifth to seventh days of the first lunar month a Water Puppet festival is held at Thay Pagoda west of Hanoi.
February/March: Fourteen days after Tet, at Lim Village, Bac Ninh Province, in the Red River Delta, *quan ho* songs are performed as men and women sing improvised lyrics of love, compliment and amiable jest.
March: On the sixth day of the second lunar month, the *Hai Ba Trung* festival honours the Trung sisters' resistance to the Chinese. At Hai Ba Trung Temple in Hanoi.
March/April: At full moon of the second lunar month pilgrims travel to Chua Huong, the Perfume Pagoda near Hanoi, for the climax of the Perfume Pagoda Festival. Eighth day of the fourth lunar month: at *Phat Dan* lanterns are hung out to celebrate the Buddha's enlightenment.
May/June: Fifth day of the fifth lunar month: *Tet Doan Ngo* signals the summer solstice. Celebrations held to ensure good health and well being. Eighth day of the fourth moon is *Dan Sinh* or the Birthday of the Buddha.
August: Fourteenth day of the seventh lunar month, *Trang Nguyen or Vu Lan* marks the Day of Lost Souls. Tombs are cleansed and offerings made to spirits.
September/October: *Kate*, or Cham New Year, at Phan Rang. Fourteenth day of the eighth lunar month, *Trung Thu* or Mid-Autumn Festival is celebrated as Children's Day with dragon dances and gifts of special cakes. Sixteenth day of eighth lunar month is the Whale Festival at Vung Tau. Crowds gather to make offerings to whales.
December: December 25: *Giang Sinh* or Christmas Day.

Taking part in the Tet

In the mood

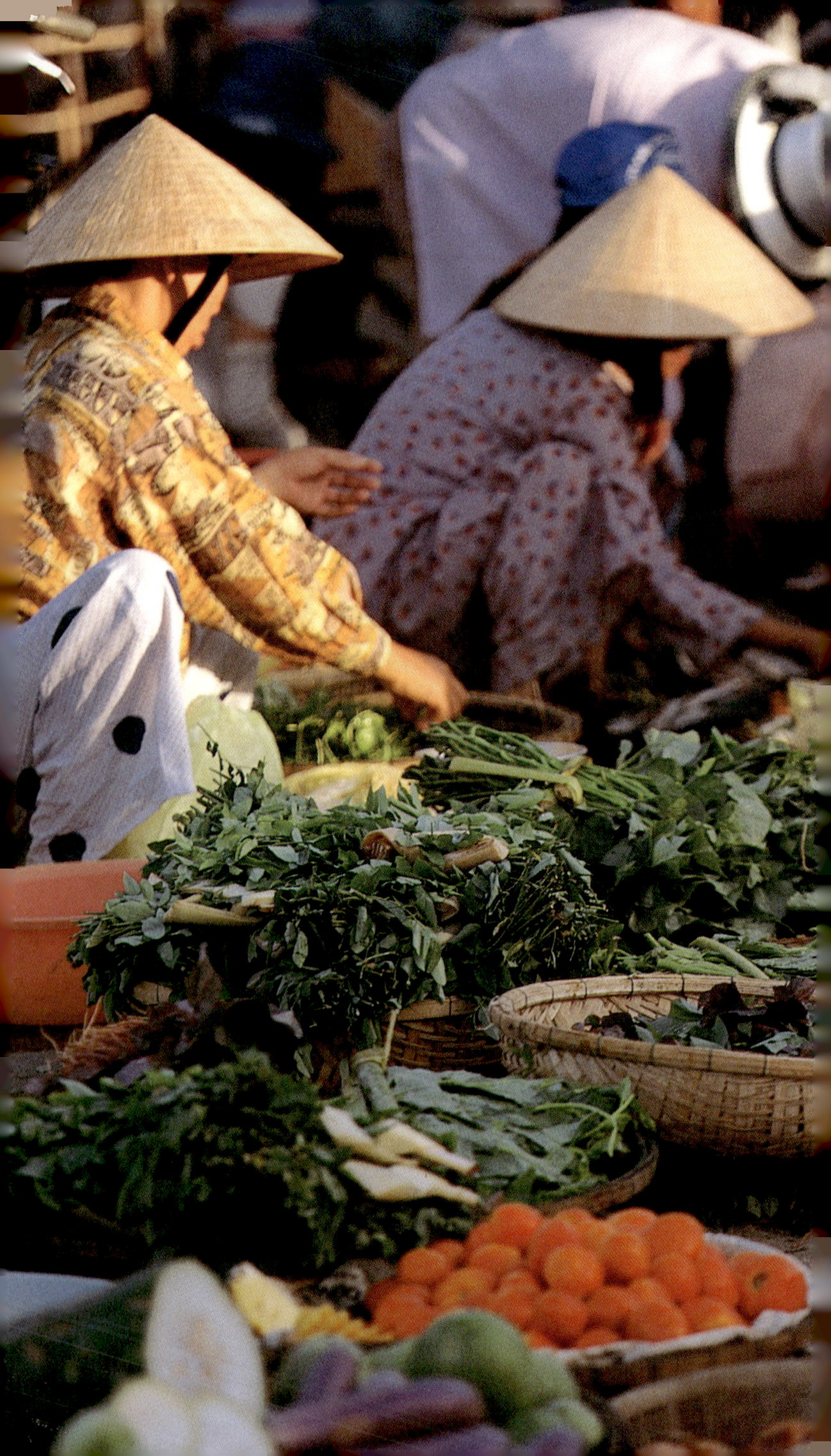

Food and Drink

Opposite: at the market in Da Nang

Like so much else in Vietnam, the cuisine reflects long years of cultural exchange with China, Cambodia and, more recently, France. As elsewhere in Southeast Asia, rice is the main staple, though bread – especially baguettes introduced by the French – is ubiquitous and usually very good. Dishes are generally served at the same time rather than by course, and eaten with long-grain rice, *nuoc mam* or fish sauce, and a wide range of fresh herbs and vegetables. Meals are generally eaten with chopsticks or, if European food, with knife and fork.

Some of the more popular Vietnamese dishes include *Cha gio* (known as *nem Saigon* in the north): small 'spring rolls' of minced pork, prawn, crabmeat, fragrant mushrooms and vegetables wrapped in thin rice paper and then deep fried. *Cha gio* is rolled in a lettuce leaf with fresh mint and other herbs, then dipped in a sweet sauce. *Chao tom* is a northern delicacy: ground up shrimp is baked on a stick of sugar cane, then eaten with lettuce, cucumber, coriander (cilantro) and mint, and dipped in fish sauce. Another dish eaten in a similar fashion is *cuon diep*, or shrimp, noodles, mint, coriander and pork wrapped in lettuce leaves.

Hue, a city associated with Buddhism, is famous for its vegetarian cuisine as well as for its *banh khoai*, or 'Hue pancake'. A batter of rice flour and corn is fried with egg to make a pancake, and then wrapped around pork or shrimp, onion, bean sprouts and mushrooms. Another popular Hue speciality is *bun bo*, or fried beef and noodles served with coriander, onion, garlic, cucumber, chilli peppers and tomato paste.

Soups are popular, and generally served with almost every meal. *Mien ga* is a noodle soup, most popular in the south, blending chicken, coriander, fish sauce and scallions. *Hu tieu* is chicken, beef, pork and shrimp served with a broth over rice noodles mixed with crabmeat, peanuts, onion and garlic. *Canh chua*, a sour soup served with shrimp or fish head, is a fragrant blend of tomato, pineapple, star fruit, bean sprouts, fried onion, bamboo shoots, coriander and cinnamon.

Perhaps the best known of all Vietnamese soup dishes, often eaten for breakfast or as a late-night snack, is *pho*, a broth of rice noodles topped with beef or chicken, fresh herbs and onion. Egg yolk is often added, as may be lime juice, chilli peppers or vinegar. *Pho* is generally served with *quay* – a fried piece of flour dough.

Fruits, desserts and drinks

A wide range of fruit is available, including many lush tropical fruits such as mango, custard apple, sapodilla,

Preparing a rice paper roll

Dishes are served at the same time

Drinking-up time

A courtyard café

The Nam Phuong

durian, pineapple, star fruit, and rambutan. More temperate fruits such as apples, cherries and strawberries can be found in the north.

Bottled fresh water, canned and bottled soft drinks and a wide range of canned beers are available throughout the country. French and Australian wines are becoming increasingly popular, especially at French restaurants. Local rice liquors are cheap and fierce; as a legacy of Vietnam's recent history, Stolychnaya and other Russian vodkas may be found on some shelves.

Restaurants

This selection from Vietnam's principal centres is listed according to the following categories: $$$ = expensive; $$ = moderate; $ = cheap.

Hanoi
Al Fresco's, 23L Hai Ba Trung, tel: 826 7782. A variety of steaks, pizzas, pastas and fresh salads. Be wary when ordering, the portions are huge. $$. **Le Beaulieu**, Sofitel Metropole, 15 Ngo Quyen, tel: 826 6919. A Vietnamese and mainly French menu. Each morning there is a large breakfast buffet with various freshly baked cakes and breads. $$$. **Cha Ca La Vong**, 14 Cha Ca Street, tel: 825 3929. They only serve fried freshwater fish, a Hanoi speciality, and it's truly excellent. There are plenty of other *Cha Ca* restaurants around town but this is the best. $$. **Il Padrino**, 42 Le Thai To Street, tel: 828 8449. A wine bar and delicatessen, well located on Hoan Kiem Lake. $$. **Indochine**, 16 Nam Ngu Street, tel: 824 6097. One of the most exclusive Vietnamese restaurants in town. You will find most of Vietnam's speciality dishes served here. $$$. **Lotus Restaurant**, 16 Ngo Quyen Street, tel: 826 7618. Mainly Vietnamese and Chinese cuisine with some Western dishes. $$. **Nam Phuong**, 19 Phan Chu Trinh, tel: 824 0926. A pleasant atmosphere in which to savour the authentic southern Vietnamese dishes. $$. **Piano Restaurant**, 50 Hang Vai Street, tel: 823 2423. Vietnamese and Chinese menu in a stylish location. Live, Western classical music on most nights. $$$. **San Ho Restaurant**, 58 Ly Thuong Kiet Street, tel: 822 2184. For great seafood look no further than this place. $$. **Seasons of Hanoi**, 95B Quan Thanh Street, tel: 843 5444. Classic Vietnamese cuisine in a beautiful French-style villa with live traditional music. $$. **Tandoor Restaurant**, 24 Hang Be Street, in the Old Quarter near the Hoan Kiem Lake, tel: 824 5359. Excellent northern Indian dishes and vegetarian curries. $$. **Thuy Ta Café**, 1 Le Thai To, tel: 828 8148. Right at the northern end of Hoan Kiem Lake. A great place to take a break and indulge in the good selection of coffee, cakes and ice cream on offer. $.

Variety at Hue Market

Tucking in

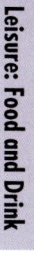

Ho Chi Minh City

Ancient Town, 211 Dien Bien Phu Street, tel: 829 9625. Specialities from all corners of the country served in a beautiful villa. $$. **Givral**, 169 Dong Khoi Street, tel: 824 2750. An extremely varied menu encompassing French, Japanese, Chinese and of course Vietnamese dishes. Also serves cakes, yoghurt and ice cream. $$. **Lemongrass**, 4 Nguyen Thiep Street, tel: 822 0496. Superb food served to the sounds of traditional Vietnamese music. $$$. **Mandarine**, 11A Ngo Van Nam Street, tel: 822 9783. A fabulous selection of traditional Vietnamese cuisine. $$. **Maxim's Dinner Theatre**, 15–17 Dong Khoi Street, tel: 829 6676. A mix of Chinese and French food. After the meal, carry on upstairs and enjoy the free nightclub. It's probably best to book ahead at the weekend. $$. **Q Bar**, City Concert Hall, 7 Lam Son Square, tel: 823 5424. The classiest bar in town. $$. **Vietnam House**, 93-95 Dong Khoi Street, tel: 829 1623. A restaurant in an old colonial villa with live music on each floor. Your choice of a four-piece traditional group or a pianist. $$$.

Hue

Hoa Mai Restaurant, 2nd Floor, Huong Giang Hotel, 51 Le Loi Street, tel:822 122. Vietnamese and Western dishes and Hue specialities including sweet soups. $$. **Lac Thien Restaurant**, Dien Tien Hoang Street, tel: 832 480. Some of the best food to be found in Hue, but the décor is almost non-existent. Try the dried noodles with beef. The staff are very friendly and provide a lively atmosphere. $. **Ong Tao**, 43 Dinh Cong Trang Street, tel: 823 031. Next to the Citadel's Hien Nhon Gate, a restaurant serving Hue specialities in a pleasant garden setting. $$. **Song Huong Floating Restaurant**, 3–2 Le Loi Street, tel: 826 655. A floating restaurant on the Perfume River next to the Trang Tien Bridge. $$. **Tinh Gia Vien**, 20–23 Le Thanh Ton

Accompaniments to seafood

Iced coffee

Street, tel: 822 243. Serves lunch and dinner in a beautiful garden setting with more than 200 bonsai trees. They serve Imperial meals with as many as 12 dishes. And if you are in the mood to dress for dinner, Imperial costume will be provided. $$.

Danang
Christie's, 2nd Floor, 9 Bach Dang Street, tel: 826 645. Set above the waters of the Han River. Serves a fine selection of Vietnamese and European food as well as some Australian specials. $$. **Songhan Restaurant**, 56B Hoang Van Thu Street, tel: 816 005. This floating restaurant next to the Cham Museum serves a wide variety of central Vietnamese dishes. The portions are enormous, so be careful when ordering. $$.

Hoi An
Nhu Y or **Mermaid Restaurant**, 2 Tran Phu Street, tel: 861 527. Vietnamese cuisine in a family atmosphere. $$.

Dalat
Thanh Thanh Restaurant, 4 Tang Bat Ho Street, tel: 821 836. Probably the best restaurant in Dalat. Excellent Vietnamese salads and other traditional dishes. $$.

Vung Tau
Ma Maison, 89 Tran Hung Dao Street, tel: 852 015. An exclusive French restaurant offering beautifully prepared dishes. $$$.

Nha Trang
Vietnam Restaurant, 23 Hoang Van Thu Street tel: 822 933. A special seafood restaurant: everything on offer is fresh from the South China Sea. $$.

Nightlife

Until 1975 Ho Chi Minh City – in its former Saigon incarnation – was a very wild place indeed, with bars, nightclubs and girls on every street corner. All this was swept away by the Communist victory, but 15 years of Stalinist orthodoxy didn't change the Saigonese very much, and nowadays there are nightclubs, discos and karaoke bars aplenty. Hanoi was always a more staid city than its southern sister, but today the capital is lightening up, though at a slower and more refined pace.

Hanoi
Apocalypse Now, 5C Hoa Ma Street, tel: 971 2783. Similar to Ho Chi Minh's original – busy, loud and very dark. Doesn't really get going until after 11pm.
Mai La Club, 23 Quang Trung Street, tel: 825 7799. The most sophisticated club in town, opens 8pm to 1am.
Metal Night Club, 57 Cua Nam Street, tel: 824 1975. A loud, lively disco with live music. There is a cover charge.
Municipal Water Puppet Theatre, 57B Dinh Tien Hoang Street (northeast end of Hoan Kiem Lake), tel: 824 9494. For a unique after-dark experience a visit to Hanoi's Water Puppet Theatre is a must for any visitor. Performances start at 8pm and last about 1 hour.
Vortex, 336 Ba Trieu Street, tel: 978 0121. A popular dance hall for both Vietnamese and foreigners.
Bao Khanh Street pubs and bars. A small night scene has grown up on this street to the northwest of Hoan Kiem Lake. Look out for the **Golden Cock Bar**, 5 Bao Khanh Street.

Hanoi's Municipal Water Puppet Theatre

Ho Chi Minh City
Apocalypse Now, 2C Thi Sach Street, tel: 824 1463. Over the past few years has built up a formidable reputation for loud music and wild times.
Bar Rolling Stones, 117 Pham Ngu Lao Street. One of the few good places in the budget traveller's area of Pham Ngu Lao.
Buffalo Blues, 72 Nguyen Du Street, tel: 822 2874. A surprisingly good jazz bar with live music in the basement.
The Municipal Theatre, Dong Khoi Street, tel: 829 1249. The programme usually changes once a week, and the entertainment can be truly eclectic.
Q Bar, Nha That Thanh Pho Square, Dong Khoi Street, tel: 829 1299. One of the city's oldest and most popular bars.
Queen Bee Disco, 104–106 Nguyen Hue Boulevard. A large disco and karaoke joint spread over four floors.
Pink Cadillac Disco, Shangri-La Complex, 1196, 3 Thang 2 Street, District 11, tel: 855 6831. This extremely lively disco at the northern edge of Cholon is part of a larger complex offering karaoke, live music and a large lounge bar.

Bar tenders in Saigon

Vietnamese hats...

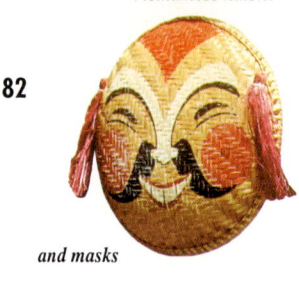

and masks

...and silk

Shopping

Painting

Vietnam is reputed to have more painters than any other Asian country. Hanoi is the centre for this activity, but Ho Chi Minh City has many fine galleries of its own. Styles vary dramatically, from traditional Vietnamese painting on silk through various modern Western schools of art. Galleries in Hanoi can be found around Hoan Kiem Lake, especially to the south and west of the lake. Hue is famous for its rice paper and silk paintings.

Antiques

Fake antiques are big business in Vietnam, and ceramics and porcelain lead the way. In Ho Chi Minh City try to avoid the tourist shops on Dong Khoi Street as prices are high. Head for the Pham Ngu Lao area where there are good antique shops and a more easy-going atmosphere. In Hanoi, bargains can be found along Hang Gai Street.

Clothing

An *ao dai* makes a good gift for a wife, sister or mother. They are relatively inexpensive and can be found in most shopping areas. Probably the best place though is the Ben Thanh Market in Ho Chi Minh City. Both Hanoi and Ho Chi Minh City have cheap T-shirts in abundance.

Hanging screens

An attractive souvenir made especially in the south and available at Ben Thanh Market is a bamboo screen designed to hang across doorways. The hundreds of tiny bamboo cylinders strung on long threads are painstakingly painted to show a typical Vietnamese theme – girls dressed in *non la* hats and *ao dai*, for example, or a blossom tree.

Active Holidays

Watersports and Diving

With such an extensive coastline, Vietnam ought to be a paradise for watersports and diving enthusiasts. Unfortunately, as yet there are very few organised activities, but as Vietnam opens to tourism this situation should improve. At the moment, the best opportunities for scuba diving and snorkelling can be found at Nha Trang, Vietnam's premier beach resort. Respected operators include the Blue Diving Club, 40 Tran Phu Street, Nha Trang, tel: 825 390.

Watersports at Nha Trang

Trekking

There are plenty of opportunities for trekking in Vietnam. Treks can be organised at various Hanoi traveller's cafés, including T.F. Handspan, 116 Pho Hang Bac Street, tel: 828 1996, fax: 825 7171, email: tfhandspn@hn.vnn.vn. Green Bamboo, 42 Nha Chung Street, tel 826 8752, fax: 826 4949, email: cuong@fpt.vn, offers tours up into the hills around Sa Pa. More upmarket and expensive tours are run by Buffalo Tours, 11 Pho Hang Muoi Street, tel 828 0702, fax 826 9370, e-mail: buffalo@netnam.org.vn

Cycling

Heading uptown

A great way to see the country is to cycle. The roads are not the best in the world, yet it is theoretically possible to cycle from Ho Chi Minh City to Hanoi. Some companies in the West offer cycling packages. One such company, in New Zealand, is Active Travel. Back-up vehicles follow you wherever you wish to go – so if you don't fancy cycling over the gruelling Hai Van Pass, just put the bicycle in the back. Active Travel is at www.active.co.nz.

Sea Kayaking

A truly unique experience is sea kayaking in and around Halong Bay. A Canadian company, Global Adventures, runs exclusive 12-day tours to Halong Bay. The tour includes various lagoons and caves, and at the end of each day accommodation is provided in the form of a traditional Vietnamese junk. This tour can be booked on the web at www.portal.ca or directly at P.O. Box 123, Delta, British Columbia, Canada V4K 3N6.

Golf

Although Vietnam is not renowned for its golf courses, there are a few good ones. Probably the finest of them is the **Cau Lac Bo Golf Club (International Golf Club of Vietnam)**, 40–42 Nguyen Trai Street, Lam Vien Park, Thu Duc District, Ho Chi Minh, tel: 832 2084, fax: 832 2083. If you're in Hanoi, try the **King's Valley Golf Club** at Dong Mo Lake, some 45km (28 miles) west of the city.

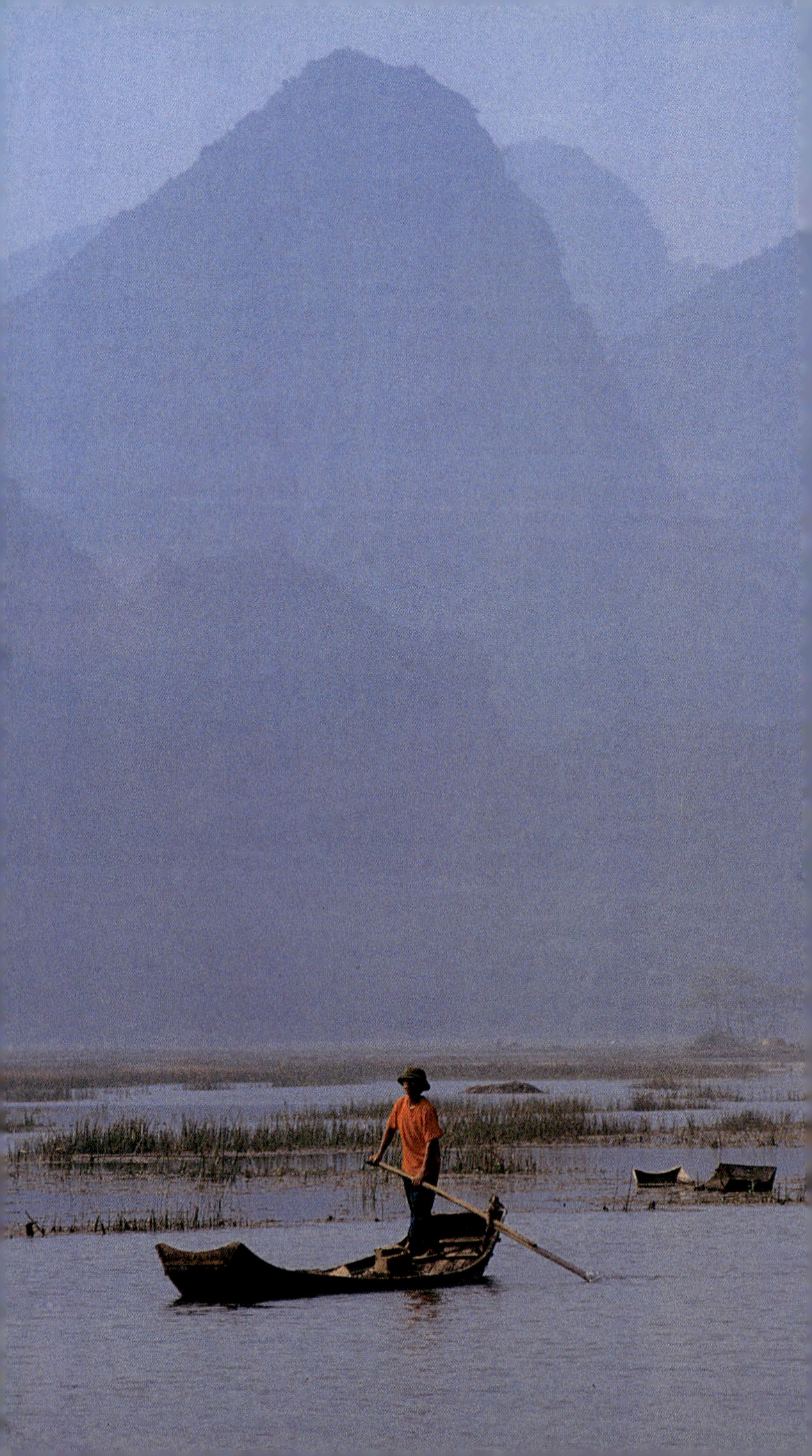

Getting There

Opposite: life on the water near Hanoi

By plane

Vietnam has two international airports, Hanoi's Noi Bai airport, and Ho Chi Minh City's Tan Son Nhat. Of the two, Tan Son Nhat is by far the busiest. Da Nang is also being developed as a regional airline entry point. There are now more than 20 international airlines servicing Vietnam with direct daily flights from Bangkok, Hong Kong, Kuala Lumpur, Phnom Penh and Singapore. Other direct flights to Noi Bai include Berlin, Dubai, Guangzhou, Moscow, Paris, Seoul, Taipei and Vientiane. Tan Son Nhat has direct links with Amsterdam, Berlin, Dubai, Frankfurt, Jakarta, Manila, Osaka, Paris, Seoul, Sydney and Taipei. It is advisable to reconfirm all your flights 72 hours before take off. A departure tax of 90,000 dong is levied for all international flights.

From the airport

Noi Bai airport is 35km from downtown Hanoi. Vietnam Airlines provides a shuttle bus service to and from its central Hanoi booking office for US$4 per person. Taxis are available in front of the Arrivals hall. A typical fare to anywhere in downtown Hanoi would be US$20. Toll charges are included in the fare.

Tan Son Nhat airport is located a mere 7 km (5 miles) or 15 minutes' drive from the heart of Ho Chi Minh City. Metered taxis are available. Fares start at about US$8.

By road

It is possible to enter Vietnam by road at various points, although none of them is to be particularly recommended. Moc Bai (Cambodia), Lao Bao (Laos), Cau Treo (Laos), Dong Dang (China) and Lao Cai (China) all involve long bus or taxi journeys. Remember that if you are entering or leaving Vietnam by any of these routes the location must be clearly stated on your visa.

By train

Trains from China enter Vietnam at the Dong Dang and Lao Cai border posts. The twice-weekly Beijing-Hanoi train uses the Dong Dang crossing. The Lao Cai entry point links Vietnam with the southwestern Chinese province of Yunnan. If you are entering or leaving Vietnam by train remember that China is one hour ahead. The China-Vietnam border closes at 4pm Vietnamese time.

By sea

The only way to enter Vietnam legally by boat is on a cruise ship. No cruise liners regularly go to Vietnam, but occasionally one will call in at Ho Chi Minh City or Da Nang. Check the major cruise lines for their schedules.

Commuter

Getting Around

By plane

Vietnam Airlines has improved greatly over the past few years. Booking offices can be found in all main towns and cities; the staff are polite and English is widely spoken. You will need to show your passport every time an air ticket is purchased. The domestic air routes are comprehensive, Vietnam Airlines flying to the following destinations: Hanoi, Ho Chi Minh City, Buon Me Thuot, Dalat, Da Nang, Dien Bien Phu, Haiphong, Hue, Nha Trang, Pleiku, Qui Nhon, Rach Gia, Tuy Hoa, and Vinh.

Vietnam does have a second domestic airline, Pacific Airlines. It does not have the same coverage as Vietnam Airlines, but can prove useful for travel between the major cities. Pacific Airlines has an all-new fleet of Boeings and Airbuses.

Domestic departure tax is 20,000 dong.

Buses tend to be overcrowded

By bus

The country has a huge bus network, but travelling this way can be extremely arduous and even quite dangerous. Roads in Vietnam are not yet up to the standards you would find in some other Southeast Asian countries. Road safety and courtesy are almost non-existent. Buses tend to be overcrowded and prone to frequent breakdowns. If you have to travel by bus it is best to do so in daylight hours as many vehicles travel without lights at night.

Train travel can be an adventure

By train

Vietnam has a reasonably extensive railway network. The main line, between Hanoi and Ho Chi Minh City, is served daily by the *Reunification Express*. The journey between the two cities usually takes between 36 and 44 hours. It is a much safer way to travel than by bus, but be careful not to leave your belongings unattended. Air-conditioned sleepers are now available and make the trip between Hanoi and Ho Chi Minh City a pleasant adventure. From Hanoi there are rail links to the Chinese border at Lao Cai and Lang Son, and also to the port city of Haiphong. Trains are usually full and so it is advisable to book well ahead of time – for a sleeping berth perhaps as much as four days in advance. Travel agencies and hotels can arrange tickets, so you will not necessarily have to go to the railway booking offices.

Taxis

Most towns and cities have more than one taxi company. Hanoi has as many as 10. All vehicles are metered and usually quite modern. Sometimes it is easier to ring the company than wait on the street for a taxi to turn up. In Hanoi

Cyclo travel in Hanoi

try Five Taxi (tel: 855 5555), Hanoi Taxi (tel: 853 5252) or Red Taxi (tel: 856 8686). Ho Chi Minh City: Festival Taxi (tel: 845 4545), Saigon Taxi (tel: 842 4242) or Vina Taxi (tel: 811 0888). Hue: Co Do Taxi (tel: 830 830).

By car

Hertz, Avis and Budget have yet to reach Vietnam. Authorities are troubled by the idea of foreigners renting and driving their own vehicles. Hotels and guesthouses can arrange cars for day trips and costs are reasonable.

Local public transport

A great way to get about most towns is in a trishaw or a cyclo. They are fairly slow, but if you have time on your hands there is no better way to see the sights. A lot of the drivers speak some English. Taking a cyclo in Ho Chi Minh City may mean a longer journey than at first anticipated as cyclos are banned from some of the larger streets and the driver will have to make certain detours.

Bicycle and motorbike hire

Hiring a motorbike to get around the big cities is only recommended to those who have some previous experience. The sheer number of motorbikes, bicycles and cars in Hanoi is overwhelming. Do not expect anyone to follow any rules, you need to just go with the flow. Fortunately traffic in Hanoi doesn't move too rapidly. Ho Chi Minh City is a different proposition, the streets are wider and things move at a much quicker pace, so great care is needed. Cafes and some hotels will rent bikes out. Be aware that it is illegal for foreigners to drive any motorbike over 125cc.

Bicycles can be rented from various cafes in Hanoi and Ho Chi Minh City. For the Imperial City of Hue a bicycle is perfect for seeing the sights as long as it is not raining.

Motorbikes for hire

Cycling is perfect for sightseeing

Exploring Halong Bay

Facts for the Visitor

Visas

A visa is essential for Vietnam, and getting one can involve quite a few hassles. It is important to state your point of entry as this will be added to the visa. You will then not be able to enter at any other point without obtaining a new visa. The time it takes to get a visa depends on where you apply for it. The Vietnamese embassy in Bangkok has a good reputation and usually takes only four days.

Customs

Duty-free allowances for each visitor are 2 litres of liquor, 200 cigarettes, and 50 cigars or 250g (8oz) of tobacco. Luggage and personal possessions in amounts sufficient for personal use.

Tourist information

Some options in Hanoi

For visa and travel information contact one of the following embassies. Australia: 6 Timbarra Crescent, O'Malley, Canberra, tel: 6286 6059, fax: 6286 4534; Canada: 25B Davidson Drive, Gloucester, Ottawa, Ontario, tel: 744 4963, fax: 744 1709; UK: 12–14 Victoria Road, London, tel: 937 1912, fax: 937 6108; USA: 1233 20th Street N.W., 20036 Washington DC, tel: 861 0737, fax: 861 0917

Currency and exchange

The Vietnamese currency is called the dong and it is used uniformly throughout the country. Bank notes in denominations of 200d, 500d, 1,000d, 2,000d, 5,000d, 10,000d, 20,000d, and 50,000d are presently in circulation. US-dollars are widely accepted at the airports, in hotels and sometimes taxi drivers will take them. Room rates are normally quoted in dollars in the better hotels, however, the government is trying to make the dong the only acceptable national currency. Only certain travellers' cheques and credit cards are acceptable in the big cities: they include. Visa, MasterCard and American Express.

Tipping

Tipping is not a traditional part of Vietnamese culture, but it is appreciated. The basic rule is that if you feel you have been well treated a small token of your gratitude would not be out of place. Hotels and top restaurants will have already added a service charge to your bill.

Time

Vietnam is seven hours ahead of Greenwich Mean Time (GMT).

Electricity

Electricity is rated at 220 volts. Sockets are of the standard European or American type.

Opening times

Banks: Monday to Friday 8am–3pm, Saturday 8am–noon.
Government offices and official bodies: Monday to Friday 8–11.30am and 2–5pm, Saturday 8am–noon..
Post offices: every day 6am–8pm.
Shops, supermarkets: daily from as early as 6am to 9pm.
Museums: usually Tuesday to Sunday, 8am–noon and 2–5pm, but check individual museums.
Temples: generally, daily 6am–6pm.
Banks, administrative offices and museums, but not post offices, are closed on all public holidays and occasionally on religious festivals.

Public holidays

Traditionally the most important festival of the year is Tet Nguyen Dan (Vietnamese Lunar New Year) or Tet for short. Officially it is three days, but many Vietnamese take a week over their celebrations. It usually falls between January and February.

These days are observed as official public holidays: January 1 (New Year's Day); February 3 (Anniversary of the founding of the Communist Party of Vietnam in 1930); March 8 (International Women's Day); March 26 (Youth Day); April 30 (*Saigon Giai Phong* or Liberation Day celebrating the fall of Saigon to communist forces on this day in 1975); May 1 (*Quoc Te Lao Dong* or International Workers' Day); May 7 (Victory over France); May 19 (*Sinh Nhat Bac Ho* or Ho Chi Minh's Birthday); June 1 (International Children's Day); July 27 (Memorial Day); August 19 (August Revolution of 1945); September 2 (*Quoc Kanh* or National Day celebrating Ho Chi Minh's procla-

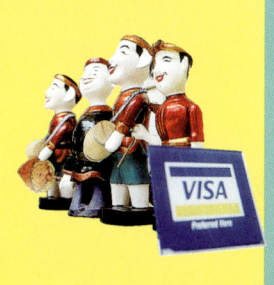

A place to get your dong

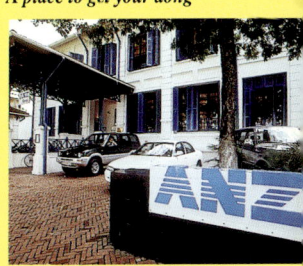

Celebration time

mation of the Declaration of Independence on this day in 1945.); November 20 (Teacher's Day); December 22 (Army Day).

Telephone, fax and email

International calls can be made from post offices and hotels. Most hotel rooms will have a telephone, but rates are very high – among the highest in the world. The hotel will also add on a hefty service charge. Ringing from the post office is cheaper, but you will be charged for the first three minutes whether you use them or not.

It is possible to send faxes from most good hotels and also post offices. However, it is illegal to hook up a fax machine to an existing telephone line. All machines have to be registered with the government, so don't go hooking up your fax modem to the hotel telephone.

Email and the Internet are still in their infancy. Some cyber cafes have set up shop in Ho Chi Minh City and Hanoi, but again the government is extremely paranoid about all this.

Keeping up communications

Etiquette

As in most Southeast Asian nations patience is a virtue. Never lose your temper, or nothing will get done. If you do have a problem, go about settling it quietly and with a smile. Always remember to remove your shoes before entering someone's house. Don't leave your chopsticks upright in a bowl of rice, it reminds Vietnamese of incense sticks burned for the dead.

Equipment and luggage

It's best not to overburden yourself with luggage. Markets in the big cities are full of cheap items if you forget anything vital. A first-aid kit for the journey should include medicines for colds, diarrhoea, upset stomach as well as adhesive plasters, insect repellent and disinfectant.

Clothing

No shorts in the pagoda

As in other mainly Buddhist countries it is best to bring shoes that are easily removable as you will have to take your shoes off before entering people's homes and some temples. In the cool season months between November and February the north of the country, especially in the mountains, can be quite cold, so bring a sweater. At times the sun can be very fierce so a sun hat is a good idea.

Photography

Film is readily available in Vietnam and at very competitive prices. Print film can be bought almost everywhere, but slide film is really only obtainable in the larger cities. Avoid buying any film from non air-conditioned shops.

Always ask permission before photographing people, especially older people. Avoid photographing anything that may have connections with the military. Certain tourist sites charge for the use of a camera, usually a nominal fee.

Health precautions

Immunisation is recommended for cholera, typhoid, tetanus and hepatitis.

Always drink bottled water, which is widely available, never tap water. Avoid eating raw vegetables and fruit without thoroughly washing and peeling them yourself.

Malarial mosquitoes are widespread in the countryside, but as long as you are staying close to the tourist areas there should be no real problems. Nevertheless it is advisable to bring along some good mosquito repellent for use on exposed skin at night. After dark it is advisable to wear long sleeved-shirts and long trousers. Consult your doctor about any recent advances in the treatment of malaria.

Health insurance

It is recommended that travellers arrange a comprehensive overseas travel sickness insurance, including transport home if necessary.

Crime

Beware of overly friendly Vietnamese offering you free drinks on long-distance buses: the drinks may be drugged. When you wake up some hours later your valuables will have been removed, and the thief will have left the bus.

Pickpockets are a problem in Ho Chi Minh City, especially around the tourist areas.

Diplomatic representation in Hanoi

Australia, Van Phuc Quarter, tel: 831 7755, fax: 831 7711.
Canada, 31 Hung Vuong Street, tel: 823 5500, fax: 823 5333.
New Zealand, 32 Hang Bai, tel: 824 1481, fax: 824 1480.
United Kingdom, 31 Hai Ba Trung Street, tel: 825 2510, fax: 826 5762.
United States, 7 Lang Ha Street, tel: 843 1500, fax: 843 1510.

Consulates in Ho Chi Minh City

Australia, 5-B Ton Duc Thang Street, District 1, tel: 829 6035, fax: 829 6024.
Canada, 203 Dong Khoi Street, Suite 102, District 1, tel: 824 2000, fax: 829 4528.
United Kingdom, 25 Le Duan Boulevard, District 1, tel: 829 8433, fax: 822 1971.
United States, 51 Nguyen Dinh Chieu Street, District 3, tel: 822 9433, fax: 822 9434.

Young visitors to Dalat

Help is at hand

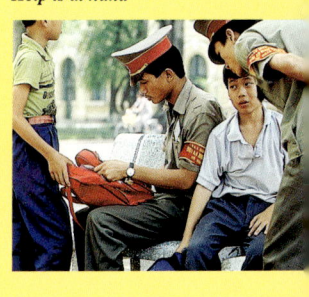

Accommodation

Accommodation in Vietnam, especially the north, has improved markedly in the past few years. But there is still some way to go before standards reach the level of neighbouring Thailand. Both Hanoi and Ho Chi Minh City offer a number of top quality hotels, but outside these areas five-star hotels are few and far between. Most hotel rooms in the big cities now offer satellite television.

The following are hotel recommendations for some of the destinations covered in this book. They fall roughly into the following price categories: $$$ = expensive; $$ = moderate; $ = inexpensive.

Far from the madding crowd

Sofitel Metropole

Hanoi
Green Park Hotel, 48 Tran Nhan Tong Street, tel: 822 7725, fax: 822 5977. Well located next to one of the biggest parks in the city. $$$. **Hanoi Horison Hotel**, 40 Cat Linh Street, tel: 733 0808, fax: 733 0888. Well located for the Temple of Literature. $$$. **Hotel Sofitel Metropole**, 15 Ngo Quyen Street, tel: 826 6919, fax: 826 6920. A truly grand, colonial-style hotel, with excellent international restaurants, it was renovated in 1992. $$$. **Melia Hanoi Hotel**, 44B Ly Thuong Kiet Street, tel: 934 3343, fax: 934 3344. The very latest luxury hotel, it even has its own heliport. $$$. **Royal Hotel**, 20 Hang Tre, tel: 824 4233, fax: 824 4234. In Hanoi's Old Quarter and not far from Hoan Kiem Lake. $$$ **Hoa Binh Hotel**, 27 Ly Thuong Street, tel: 825 3515, fax: 826 9818. Old colonial-style hotel with two good restaurants. $$. **Thuy Tien**, 1C Tong Dan Street, tel: 824 4775, fax: 824 4784. One of many new, reasonably priced hotels near the centre of the old Hanoi. $$. **Especen**, 79E Hang Trong, tel: 826 6856, fax: 826 9612. This is a chain of small inns in the Old Quarter. $. **Green Bamboo**, 42 Nha Chung, tel: 826 8752, fax: 826 4949. Some of the cheapest accommodation in the city. Provides useful travel information. $. **New World Hotel**, 21 Chau Long, tel/fax: 829 2815. Situated to the north of the city, near the Truc Bach and West lakes. $.

The Continental

Ho Chi Minh City
Continental, 132–134 Dong Khoi, tel: 829 9201, fax: 824 1772. Graham Greene's favourite, he used it as a setting for *The Quiet American*. $$$. **Majestic Hotel**, 1 Dong Khoi, tel: 829 5512, fax: 829 5510. A great location next to the Saigon River. $$$. **New World Hotel**, 76 Le Lai Street, tel: 822 8888, fax: 823 0710. By far the largest hotel in Ho Chi Minh City it has every possible convenience. $$$. **Omni Saigon Hotel**, 251 Nguyen Van Troi, Phu Nhuan District, tel: 844 9222, fax: 845 5234. Situated close to Tan Son Nhat International Airport. Rooms start

at US$180. $$$. **Rex Hotel**, 141 Nguyen Hue Boulevard, tel: 829 2186, fax: 829 6536. Has a very popular rooftop restaurant. $$$. **Saigon Prince Hotel**, 63 Nguyen Hue Boulevard, tel: 822 2999, fax: 824 1888. An international class hotel with 64 rooms and suites and great accesss to the central district. $$$. **Sofitel Plaza Saigon**, 17 Le Duan Boulevard, tel: 824 1555, fax: 823 5447. Large, new luxury hotel near Notre Dame Cathedral. $$$. **Windsor Saigon Hotel**, 193 Tran Hung Dao, tel: 836 7848, fax: 836 7889. Large rooms and an excellent bakery. $$$. **Lotus Hotel**, 117–123 Dong Khoi Street, tel: 829 1516, fax: 829 8076. This place is also known as the Bong Sen and is conveniently located near the central shopping district. $$. **Delta Caravelle Hotel**, 19–23 Lam Son Square, tel: 829 3704, fax: 829 6767. A very French feel. Has recently been extended. $$. **Oscar Saigon Hotel**, 68 Nguyen Hue Boulevard, tel: 823 1818, fax: 822 2958. Well located in Saigon's central district. $$. **Pham Ngu Lao**. This area roughly 1 kilometre (half a mile) to the west of Ho Chi Minh City's central shopping area is full of cheap accommodation and gets bigger all the time. At present there are nearly 100 small hotels and guesthouses.$.

The Rex

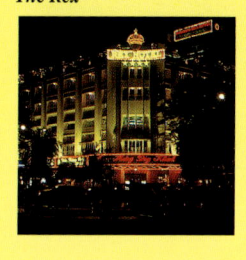

Hue
Century Riverside, 49 Le Loi Street, tel: 823 390, fax: 823 399. Luxury place with a great view of the Perfume River. $$$. **Huong Giang Hotel** (Perfume River), 51 Le Loi Street, tel: 822 122, fax: 823 102. Again overlooking the river with an excellent terrace restaurant, and its own private jetty. $$$. **Hotel Saigon Morin**, 30 Le Loi Street, tel: 823 526, fax: 825 155. Recently completely refurbished. The courtyard restaurant is very good. $$$. **Thuan Hoa Hotel,** 7 Nguyen Tri Phuong, tel: 822 553, fax: 822 470. Situated in the southeastern part of the city, with its own restaurant and terrace cafe. $$. **Thanh Noi Hotel**, 3 Dang Dung Street, tel: 822 478, fax: 827 211. A pleasant one-storey hotel located on a very quiet street close to The Citadel. $.

Da Nang
Furama Hotel, China Beach, 68 Ho Xuan Huong Street, tel: 847 333, fax: 847 666. This luxury hotel is situated in-between My Khe Beach and China Beach. $$$. **Bach Dang Hotel**, 50 Bach Dang Street, tel: 823 649, fax: 821 659. Overlooks the river. $$. **Elegant Hotel**, 22A Bach Dang Street, tel: 892 893, fax: 835 179. A comfortable new hotel, close to the Han River. $$. **Hai Au Hotel**, 177 Tran Phu Street, tel: 822 722, fax: 824 165. A bright, new hotel, located close to the centre of town. $$. **Non Nuoc Hotel**, 10 Ly Thuong Kiet, Hua Nghi, tel: 821 470, 822 137. Located at the foot of the Marble Mountains and next

Practical Information: Accommodation

93

Opposite: arriving in style

to China Beach it is 14 km (9 miles) from Da Nang. A beautiful place to rest. Advance booking advised. $$.

Dalat
Sofitel Dalat Palace Highland, Da Lat Palace, 12 Tran Phu Street, tel: 825 444, fax: 825 666. Beautifully situated an, one of the great old hotels of Southeast Asia. Built in 1922, it offers wonderful views of Xuan Huong Lake. Even if you are not staying here, visit the bar to soak up the atmosphere. $$$. **Anh Dao Hotel**, 50–52 Hoa Binh Square, tel: 822 384. Very good value with lovely rooms. $$. **Minh Tam Villas**, 20A Khe Sanh Street, tel: 822 447. The house and villas are 3km (2 miles) from the town centre and afford great views of the surrounding forests and hills. $$. **Ngoc Lan Hotel**, 42 Nguyen Chi Thanh Street, tel: 822 136, fax: 824 032. A large, comfortable old hotel near the lake. $$. **Mimosa Hotel**, 170 Phan Dinh Phung Street, tel: 822 656. Basic, but well maintained. $. **Thanh Binh Hotel**, 41 Nguyen Thi Minh Khai Street, tel: 822 909. Opposite the bustling central market. $.

Halong Bay
Heritage Hotel, 88 Halong Road, tel: 846 888, fax: 846 718. Probably the best place in Halong Bay. $$$. **Halong Bay Hotel**, Bai Chay Beach, tel: 845 209, fax: 846 856. A popular place for tour groups. $$. **Vuon Dao Hotel**, Bai Chay Beach, tel: 846 427, fax: 846 287. A large state-run hotel, slightly away from the beach. $$.

Vung Tau
Phuong Dong Hotel, 2 Thuy Van, tel: 852 593. One of the best places on Back Beach. $$. **Pacific Hotel**, 4 Le Loi Street, tel: 856 740, fax: 852 391. Unusually, it has a very good Czech restaurant. $$. **Sea Breeze Hotel**, 11 Nguyen Trai Street, tel: 856 392, fax: 856 856. Situated to the southern end of Front Beach. $$.

Hoi An
Hoi An Hotel, 6 Tran Hung Dao Street, tel: 861 373. A large, grand old place. $$. **Vinh Hung Hotel**, tel: 861 621. Not far from the old Japanese Covered Bridge. $.

Nha Trang
Ana Mandara Resort, Tran Phu Street, tel: 829 829, fax: 829 629. A series of splendid villas overlooking the sea. Already being voted one of the great resorts of Southeast Asia. $$$. **Nha Trang Lodge**, 42 Tran Phu Street, tel: 810 500, fax: 828 800. A high-rise luxury hotel, all rooms face what is probably the best beach in Vietnam. $$$. **Hai Yen Hotel**, 40 Tran Phu Street, tel: 822 828, fax: 821 902. Another large hotel facing the beach. $$.

Hotel Room in Nha Trang

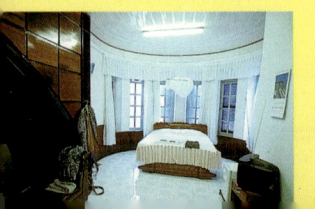

Index

A
- Acccommodation....92–4
- Anh Binh Island..........70

B
- Ba Tu Long Bay..........37
- Bai Chai......................36
- Bat Treng.................33–4
- Buddhism......................9
- But Thap Pagoda........34

C
- Cai Be floating market.........70
- Cai Rang floating market.........70
- Can Tho......................70
- Cao Dai religion 10, 67–8
- Cat Ba National Park ..37
- Cha Ban......................57
- Cham Museum............51
- Cham Towers........56, 57
- Chams...........8, 10, 54–5
- Chau Doc.................70–1
- Chien Dang Cham.......56
- China Beach................51
- Christianity..................10
- Chua Hong (Perfume Pagoda).....33
- Chua Soc Son..............34
- climate..........................7
- Co Loa.........................31
- Confucianism................9
- Cu Chi Tunnels...........67
- cuisine.....................77–8
- cycling.........................83

D
- Da Nang......................51
- Dalat........................58–9
- Deo Hai Van............49–51
- Dien Bien Phu.............40
- Do Son beach..............36
- Dong Ky.....................34

E
- Economy.................13–14
- environment...........14–15
- ethnic groups................8

F
- Fansipan.....................40
- festivals......................75

G
- Geography.................6–7
- golf.............................83

H
- Haiphong..................35–6
- Halong Bay.............36–7
- Hanoi......................20–30
  - Army Museum............27
  - Chua Quan Su...........30
  - Cot Co Flag Tower...27
  - Dao Quan Bich Cau...29
- Den Bach Ma Temple..................23
- Den Ngoc Son......23–4
- Dong Xuan Market...22
- Hanoi Hilton.............30
- History Museum.......30
- Ho Chi Minh's House 26
- Ho Chi Minh Mausoleum............26
- Ho Chi Minh Museum..................27
- Ho Hoan Kiem..........21
- Long Bien Bridge.....23
- Martyrs' Monument .24
- National Fine Arts Museum..................27
- Old Quarter...........21–3
- One Pillar Pagoda....26
- Opera House............30
- Presidential Palace...26
- Quan Thanh Temple.25
- Residence of the Governor of Tonkin 30
- St Joseph's Cathedral................21
- Temple of Literature (Van Mieu)........27–9
- Tran Quoc Pagoda....25
- Water Puppet Theatre...................24
- West Lake.................25
- Writing Brush Pillar.23
- history.......12–13, 16–17
- Ho Chi Minh City .60–65
  - Art Museum..............64
  - Ben Thanh Market....64
  - Binh Tay Market.......64
  - Cholon (Chintown) 64–5
  - Cholon Mosque.........65
  - Chua Ngoc Huang....61
  - Giac Lam Pagoda.....65
  - Giac Vien Pagoda....65
  - History Museum...63–4
  - Military Museum......62
  - Nghia An Hoi Quan Pagoda..................65
  - Notre Dame Cathedral................61
  - Revolutionary Museum..................62
  - Tam Son Hoi Quan Pagoda..................65
  - Thien Hau Pagoda ...65
  - War Remnants Museum..............61–2
  - Waterfront................60
  - Xa Loi Pagoda..........61

- Ho Than Tho (Lake of Sighs).........59
- Hoa Binh......................40
- Hoa Hao movement............10, 71
- Hoa Lu........................33
- Hoi An.....................51–2
- Hong Gai.....................36
- Hue..............................41
  - Cot Co Flag Tower...41
  - Cua Ngo Mon (Meridian Gate) 42
  - Cuu Dinh (Dynastic Urns).....................45
  - Ho Quyen (Royal Arena)........48
  - Hoang Thanh (Yellow . Imperial City)....43–4
  - Imperial Museum.....45
  - Kinh Thanh (citadel)..............42–5
  - Nam Giao Dan (Altar of Heaven) ..46
  - Nine Holy Cannons ..42
  - Perfume River..........48
  - Phu Cat (Merchants' Quarter).................45
  - Temple of Literature (Van Mieu) 46
  - Thai Binh Lau (Royal Library)......44
  - Thai Hoa Dien.........43
  - The Mieu..................45
  - Thien Mu Pagoda 45
  - Tombs of the Nguyen Emperors............46–8
  - Tu Cam Thanh (Forbidden Purple City)...................44–5

I
- Islam...........................10

K
- Khuong My..................56

L
- Lai Chau.....................40
- Lan Ha Bay.................37
- language.................10–12
- Lao Kai.......................38
- Lat Village..................59
- Long Xuyen................70

M
- Marble Mountains.......51
- Mekong Delta.........69–71
- minorities..................8–9
- Museum of the Nationalities of Vietnam..................34

- My Lai........................56
- My Son........................55
- My Tho........................69

N
- Nha Trang...................57
- nightlife......................81
- Nui Ba Den.................68

P
- Pan Thiet....................57
- people.......................8–9
- Phong Dien floating market.........70
- Po Klong Garai Cham Towers..........57
- Po Nagar Cham Towers....................57
- politics...................12–13
- Prenn Falls.................59

Q
- Qui Nhon..................56–7

R
- Religion...................9–10
- restaurants.............78–80

S
- Saigon
  - *see* Ho Chi Minh City
- Sapa........................38–9
- sea kayaking...............83
- shopping.....................82
- So...............................34
- Son La........................40
- Song Hong (Red River Valley).....................38

T
- Taoism.....................9–10
- Tay Hong Pagoda........33
- Tay Ninh.................67–8
- temple architecture......73
- Thai Nguyen...............34
- Than That (Cao Dai Great Temple)..........68
- Thap Doi.....................57
- Thay Pagoda...............33
- theatre........................74
- Tram Ton Pass............40
- tourist information......87
- transport.................85–7
- trekking......................83

V
- Van Phong Bay...........57
- Van Phuc....................34
- Vinh Long...............69–70
- Vung Tau.................66–7

W
- Water puppetry...........74
- watersports.................83
- wildlife.......................15

© APA Publications GmbH & Co. Verlag KG Singapore Branch, Singapore.